"I wear the colours of the little royal maid."

— Robert Louis Stevenson

PRINCESS KA'IULANI

Hope of a Nation,
Heart of a People

SHARON LINNÉA

EERDMANS BOOKS FOR YOUNG READERS
GRAND RAPIDS, MICHIGAN / CAMBRIDGE, U.K.

© 1999 by Sharon Linnéa Scott
Published 1999 by
Eerdmans Books for Young Readers
an imprint of
Wm. B. Eerdmans Publishing Co.
255 Jefferson Ave. S.E., Grand Rapids, Michigan 49503 /
P.O. Box 163, Cambridge CB3 9PU U.K.

Printed in the United States of America

03 02 01 00 99   7 6 5 4 3 2 1

Library of Congress Cataloging-in-Publication Data

Linnéa, Sharon.
Princess Ka'iulani: hope of a nation, heart of a people / by Sharon Linnéa.
p.   cm.
Includes bibliographical references and index.
ISBN 0-8028-5145-2 (cloth: alk. paper)
ISBN 0-8028-5088-X (pbk.: alk. paper)
1. Kaiulani, Princess of Hawaii, 1875-1899 — Juvenile literature.
2. Princesses — Biography — Juvenile literature.
3. Hawaii — History — Juvenile literature.   I. Title.
DU627.17.K3L56   1999
996.9'02'092 — dc21

[B]   97-14260
                                                          CIP

For my parents, William Diderichsen Webber
and Marilynn Carlson Webber,
who taught me that books can make real
a time and place gone by.

For those of Hawaiian heritage
who proudly preserve their culture.

For all who love Ka'iulani's beautiful islands
and seek to live in the true spirit of aloha.

And for my princess, Linnéa Juliet Scott.

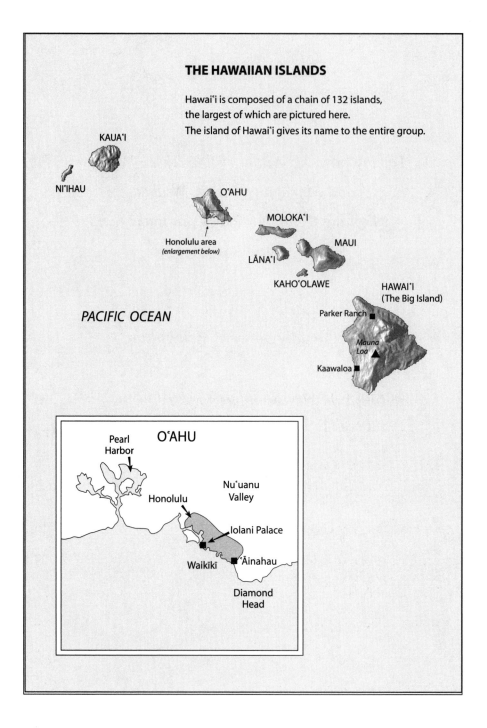

THE HAWAIIAN ISLANDS

Hawai'i is composed of a chain of 132 islands,
the largest of which are pictured here.
The island of Hawai'i gives its name to the entire group.

KAUA'I

NI'IHAU

O'AHU

MOLOKA'I

Honolulu area
(enlargement below)

LĀNA'I

MAUI

KAHO'OLAWE

HAWAI'I
(The Big Island)

Parker Ranch ■

*Mauna
Loa* ▲

Kaawaloa ■

PACIFIC OCEAN

O'AHU

Pearl
Harbor

Nu'uanu
Valley

Honolulu

Iolani Palace

Waikīkī

'Āinahau

Diamond
Head

Contents

CONTENTS

Acknowledgments

It seems fitting to open with a word of gratitude. First, I thank two knowledgeable and gracious historians, R. Kawika Makanani of the Kamehameha School and Holly McEldowney of Hawaii's State Historic Preservation Division, for their eye-opening discussions of the continually evolving interpretations of Hawaii's past. I owe a great debt to each for their input, especially on the presentation of the islands' history in Chapter One.

On a more personal note, thanks to Lorrie Lazar, without whom no words would appear on these pages, and to Jenny Lazar, who gave the manuscript an early read through a teenager's eyes.

Thanks to Mary Ann O'Roark for suggestions and support every step of the way, and to my wonderful husband, Robert Scott, my anchor in every storm.

Thanks, too, to all those who recognized the importance of Ka'iulani's story: Susan Cohen, a sane voice in a crazy profession, who has somehow become the official agent of Princess Ka'iulani; to

Amy DeVries for commissioning this book, Mary Hietbrink for strengthening it, Judy Zylstra for standing behind it, and Gayle Brown and Klaas Wolterstorff for the special design.
Mahalo Nui!

A Word about the Hawaiian Language

If you've ever heard Hawaiian, you know that it's a dramatic and expressive language. The language is meant to be spoken; in fact, no written version existed until the missionaries arrived in the islands less than two hundred years ago.

The entire Hawaiian alphabet consists of only twelve letters: the English vowels *a, e, i, o,* and *u;* and seven consonants, *h, k, l, m, n, p,* and *w.* Here is a very simplified guide to pronunciation.

The consonants retain their American sounds.

The vowels are generally pronounced as follows:

a   is *uh* (as in amount)
ā   is *ah* (as in ha)
e   is *eh* (as in led)
ē   is *ay* (as in hey)
i   is *ee* (as in piece)
o   is *oh* (as in oboe)
u   is *oo* (as in blue)

When you see a macron (ˉ) over a vowel, it not only changes the sound; it alerts you to give the vowel a little more emphasis, to draw it out a bit.

Also important is the glottal stop, which looks like an inverted comma (ʻ). The glottal stop cues you to do just that — stop briefly in the middle of the word, then keep going. It's much like the English "uh-oh."

In Hawaiian, unlike English, there are no tricky instances where vowels or consonants run together, although sometimes two vowels will be said quickly together, almost like an English diphthong. For example, the word *poi* is usually spoken as one syllable, though each vowel briefly gets its own sound.

Four basic rules will take you far in pronouncing Hawaiian:

1. Each letter gets a sound.
2. There is never more than one consonant per syllable.
3. Every syllable ends with a vowel. So it's easy to sound out "Honolulu": Ho-no-lu-lu. If you can do that, you can do it with longer, harder-looking words, like Ka-wā-na-na-ko-a.
4. The final rule of thumb is that words are accented on their *second-to-last syllable.* So: Ka-i-u-LA-ni. (Kah-ee-oo-LA-nee). Words with only two syllables are accented on the first syllable. So: LE-i (LAY-ee).

A final interesting note is that during the time period which this book discusses, Hawaiians often found it in their best interests to seem Westernized. Consequently, they seldom used correct Hawaiian punctuation while writing, leaving out glottal stops and macrons. During her life, Princess Kaʻiulani spelled her name simply "Kaiulani" and let it be pronounced in the Anglicized way: Kaye-oo-LA-nee.

In recent times, as native Hawaiian pride and culture have flourished once again, the written language has been restored, treated with proper respect, and so it is again punctuated correctly — which also gives foreigners a much easier guide to pronunciation!

Here are pronunciations of some of the Hawaiian words used in this book:

Āinahau (āy-NA-how): "Land of Cool Breezes," the name of Ka'iulani's Waikīkī estate

ali'i (uh-LEE-ee): chief; the highest nobility (Like other nouns in the Hawaiian language, the plural form does not take an "s.")

aloha (ah-LOW-ha): "love"; a wish spoken both in greeting and in parting

anaana (ah-na-AH-na): the ancient pray-to-death ritual

haole (HOW-lee): a Caucasian foreigner; the term is slightly derogatory

holokū (ho-LO-koō): a long Hawaiian dress with a yoke and a train; it can be made to be casual or very dressy

Huna (HOO-nah): the ancient Hawaiian religion; literally "The Secret"

'Iolani (ee-o-LAH-nee): "The Hawk of Heaven," the name of the royal palace

kāhili (kūh-HEE-lee): large sticks decorated with colorful feathers, symbols of Hawaiian royalty

kahuna (ka-HOO-nah): a scholar or priest

Ka'iulani (ka-ee-oo-LAH-nee): the last crown princess of Hawai'i

Kalākaua (ka-lah-KOW-ah): the last king of Hawai'i

Kamehameha (ka-MAY-ha-MAY-ha): the great warrior who united the islands; the dynasty he founded is named after him

kanaka (ka-NAH-ka): a person (typically used to refer to a commoner, someone not of the ali'i class)

Kapi'olani (kah-pee-o-LAH-nee): Kalākaua's queen

kapu (KA-poo): forbidden, sacred — also used to describe the laws that defined the sacred or forbidden

keiki (KEHee-kee): child

lānai (lah-NA-ee, or la-NYE): an open-air living space; a veranda

lei (LAY-ee): a wreath of flowers

Likelike (lee-kay-LEE-kay): Ka'iulani's mother

Lili'uokalani (lee-lee-u-oh-kah-LAH-nee): Hawai'i's last queen

lū'au (loo-AHoo): a great feast

mō'ī (MOH-EE): the king

nei (NAYee): this very place

nui (NOOee): big, large, grand

paniolo (pah-nee-O-low): cowboy

poi (POHee): a white paste made from mashed taro, a native plant

Prologue

The mood on the New York City pier that chilly first day of March was one of expectation. Reporters clutched their pencils and notebooks, waiting to get the scoop and rush back to their papers; others had come purely out of curiosity. For on board the giant oceanliner *Teutonic,* arriving from England, was an actual barbarian princess.

At least, that's what Americans had been led to believe.

Only five weeks before, in January of 1893, a momentous event had occurred in the faraway island nation of Hawaiʻi. A political coalition, headed by American businessmen, had overthrown the country's government and deposed the queen. The businessmen had quickly sent representatives to Washington with the news, suggesting that Congress quickly annex the islands to the United States.

The revolutionaries pointed out the economic boon this would bring, with rich sugar profits to be made. Perhaps more important, the islands were located strategically for military purposes. Yes, the

Hawaiian government had always been friendly to the U.S. government, but the representatives claimed that Hawaiian monarchs could not be trusted. They were childish, uneducated, and savage. When the Hawaiian king had visited the United States several years earlier, one newspaper had drawn him as a caricature of an African, boiling missionaries in a large cauldron.

The representatives spoke to every newspaper they could. Who knew when these heathen might revoke American trade privileges? they asked. In January the current queen had attempted to establish a new constitution — one that gave native Hawaiians as many rights as Westerners! Who could tell what she'd try next? It was for the good of American business investments — in fact, for the good of the childlike, heathen natives themselves — that the United States should take over.

Now the queen's niece, who was next in line for the throne — the barbarian princess with the exotic name of Kaʻiulani — was arriving in person to ask Congress to restore her nation to her people. The assembled crowd chattered in anticipation. What would she look like? What would she wear? How would she behave?

Then, almost unexpectedly, a young woman stood before them. She was tall and slender with large, dark eyes. Her dress was the latest style, a simple gray gown covered with a dark jacket; her long black hair was swept up under a Parisian bonnet. As she stood studying the crowd, it was as if they stifled a collective gasp.

She was beautiful.

Without looking, Kaʻiulani knew that her guardian, Theophilus Davies, was at her side; in fact, most of the Davies family stood behind her, their encouragement sending her forward. Less than six months ago, she'd been laughing about her "comportment" lessons, giggling with her friends about how to enter a room correctly.

Now she, who had never done any public speaking, was facing a crowd of reporters. She was terrified, but she was determined not to let it show. There was so much at stake!

She felt strongly that God was with her, giving her strength. When she looked out at the sea of faces, in her mind's eye she no longer saw New Yorkers, strangers — but her own people, Hawaiians.

"Speak for us!" they urged.

With new courage, the young woman stood straight. In a strong, refined voice laced with a soft English accent, she said:

Unbidden I stand upon your shores today, where I had thought so soon to receive a royal welcome. I come unattended except for the loving hearts that come with me over the winter seas. I hear the commissioners [representatives] from my land have been for many days asking this great nation to take away my little vineyard. They speak no word to me, and leave me to find out as I can from the rumors of the air that they would leave me without a home or a name or a nation.

Seventy years ago, Christian America sent over Christian men and women to give religion and civilization to Hawai'i. Today three of the sons of those missionaries are at your capitol, asking you to undo their fathers' work. Who sent them? Who gave them the authority to break the constitution which they swore they would uphold?

Today I, a poor, weak girl, with not one of my people near me and all these statesmen against me, have the strength to stand up for the rights of my people. Even now I can hear their wail in my heart, and it gives me strength and I am strong . . . strong in the faith of God, strong in the knowledge that I am right, strong in the strength of seventy million people who in this free land will hear my cry and will refuse to let their flag cover dishonor to mine!"

The reporters got their story. The Hawaiian princess was not a barbarian at all — in fact, she had been taught at the best English schools. She spoke not only fluent English and Hawaiian, but French and German as well. Moreover, she wasn't a "heathen," but a Christian. It seemed there was another side to this Hawaiian issue, new questions to be asked. Within the week, these new questions would be asked all the way to the White House.

Meanwhile, the newly anointed stateswoman escaped gratefully into her carriage. She knew her attempt to change history had just begun.

At the time, Kaʻiulani was seventeen years old.

PRINCESS KAʻIULANI

An early view of Honolulu, looking inland.
This is the Hawaiʻi that Western influence changed forever.

ONE

Two Worlds Collide

Things had seemed much different once. Ka'iulani's nation had belonged to her people, and her place in its future had been assured.

Monday, February 12, 1883, was a day the then seven-year-old princess would remember all her life. That morning, as she came into town in the shining carriage with her parents, the streets of Honolulu were teeming with life. In fact, so many thousands of people were arriving that it was soon difficult to get anywhere near the palace. Everyone — Hawaiians and Westerners alike — was coming to see the coronation of the king.

Ka'iulani's uncle, Kalākaua, had already been king for nine years. Recently he had become the first reigning monarch of any nation to circumnavigate the globe. He had visited the courts and parliaments of many nations, making political friends for Hawai'i, finding contract laborers for its sugar plantations, making economic treaties. He had witnessed the court life of the emperor of Japan,

King Kalākaua, the
"Merrie Monarch,"
in full regalia

heard the waltzes of Vienna, seen the crown jewels and castles of Britain.

When he returned home, he was ready to make the Hawaiian monarchy a world-class institution. He had already commissioned and had built a new, regal palace to replace the old wooden house where former kings had lived. Today he would be the first Hawaiian king to be formally crowned in a lavish ceremony. Hawai'i would take its place proudly among the modern nations.

For as long as she could remember, Ka'iulani had understood

that she was a princess. Still, the throngs of subjects, the shimmering excitement that wove through the morning air, how breathtakingly beautiful her mother looked in her white brocaded gown trimmed with precious pearls — and how regal Ka'iulani felt herself, in her pale blue dress of silk "corded and trimmed with lace," the matching ribbons in her flowing black hair — it all nearly overwhelmed her. The Hawaiian flag — red, white, and blue stripes with a Union Jack in the upper corner — flew everywhere. As their carriage rolled within sight of 'Iolani Palace, Ka'iulani caught her breath. The handsome building was awash in bunting. Large *lānai* surrounded both stories, a tower rose at each of the building's four corners, and two larger ones sat at each side of the entrance. The wide front stairs and the graceful pillars made it truly look like a "hawk of heaven," which is what its name meant.

Today there was a large coronation pavilion in front of the palace, in which sat two royal thrones. The Royal Band was already playing; rousing numbers were interspersed with Hawaiian chants recalling the noble birth and life of the king.

The day would live in Ka'iulani's memory as a series of vivid images and emotions. The wait inside the palace, with the anticipation becoming nearly unbearable. Then the coronation procession itself, and her own place in it. The services read in both English and Hawaiian; her cousins carrying the crowns; her mother draping the cape of Kamehameha around the shoulders of her uncle, the king; King Kalākaua crowning himself and his queen. The regal uniforms of ship captains and delegates from many countries of the world. Hawaiians in their best suits and holokū; Western ladies in their finest fashions from New York and Paris, preening even as they complained about the cost of the ceremonies. The *aloha* in the eyes of the subjects as they stood, proudly singing the national anthem, written by Kalākaua himself: *Hawai'i Pono'ī, Nana i kou mō'ī, Kalani*

The coronation ceremony of King Kalākaua and Queen Kapiʻolani

aliʻi, Ke aliʻi ("Hawaiʻi's own people, Be loyal to your king and queen, Heaven's appointed chiefs, The aliʻi"). Finally, at the end of the ceremony, the guns firing their salute, and the choir bursting forth with "Cry Out, O Isles, with Joy!"

But for Kaʻiulani, the best part was yet to come: the coronation ball. The pressure of the formal ceremonies was over; the night would be magic. She stalwartly endured the royal receiving line, standing proudly, accepting curtsies and acknowledgments of "Your Highness" as she'd practiced with her governess, Miss Barnes.

Then — then all around her were lights and music. The king looked dashing in his uniform, the queen exquisite in her European gown of velvet. There were squeals and laughter as the unexpected rain started, and the guests were quickly moved from the tent pavilions into the throne room. There the dancing began again, the musicians regrouping quickly on the adjacent lānai.

6

The "new" — and far more lavish — ʻIolani Palace,
built by King Kalākaua after his world travels

Kaʻiulani would always remember this special evening. How lovely her mother was in a shimmery silk gown of "moonlight on the lake" as she floated with partner after partner through the gavottes and the waltzes. How handsome her father looked! And how proud her cousin by marriage, fourteen-year-old Koa, was as he chose his first dance partners. From the sidelines, she imagined what fun she would have when she was the queen, and the coronation day was hers!

But Kaʻiulani's deepest joy came from the proud heritage that had brought the island kingdom to this night — and to the limitless possibilities of its future. Best of all, in the mind of the sleepy princess, was the unhesitating love she had received from the people, love which she had fully returned.

It was truly a day that Kaʻiulani would never forget. She under-

7

Beautiful, exotic Hawaiʻi, before explorers — and exploitation — altered the course of its history

stood as never before that the destiny of this country, these people, was inextricably interwoven with her own.

*   *   *

THE STORY OF Kaʻiulani's country, and therefore her story, started long before she was born.

Centuries earlier, the Hawaiian Islands were thrust from the restless sea by the fury of volcanos. A tiny constellation of islands in a vast sky of ocean, they matured into their mystical beauty. Towering mountains dropped off into sheer cliffs; waterfalls leapt playfully from ledge to ledge. Sometimes the sea kissed the land along sandy white beaches; sometimes it pounded against the harsh rock of black lava. Fifteen original species of birds that found a home there evolved into seventy, many unique to Hawaiʻi — from the brilliant, orange-red *iʻiwi*, to the foot-long *ʻoʻo*, with sunfire yellow feather tufts under each wing, to the *nene,* the Hawaiian goose. Eventually the brilliantly colored shallow-water fish — the parrot fish, the butterfly fish, and the clownish triggerfish — arrived to play among the coral reefs; whales made annual pilgrimages; and sharks found homes in the caves beneath the coral.

The islands remained uninhabited by humans for centuries. No one knows exactly when the first canoes arrived. Their occupants — probably from the Marquesas Islands or Tahiti, possibly from other Pacific islands — were either fleeing war or seeking adventure. If their canoes had passed a few miles further to the east or west, those aboard would certainly have died in a world of endless water. As it turned out, they discovered their own New World and founded a civilization in the North Pacific.

These first Hawaiians adapted and refined the culture and beliefs they brought with them. For example, they believed the *ali'i,* their ruling class, were descended from the gods. Because of this, the ali'i had much greater *mana,* or power, than *maka'āinana* — the ordinary citizens. The common folk fell prostrate whenever a high ali'i passed. This was prudent; if a maka'āinana so much as stepped on the shadow of a high ali'i, he or she faced immediate death. On the other hand, it was the duty of the ali'i to care for those under them. Any ruler whose people were not well fed, housed, and cared for would be shamed.

Religion was an integral part of everyday life. In many ways, *Huna* (as it came to be called in later centuries; it means "The Secret") was an advanced spiritual and psychological system. The educated class, called *kahuna,* or experts, were learned astronomers, priests, historians, and physicians. At its best, Huna taught the Hawaiians to respect the mana present in all creation and to develop a lifestyle shaped by and in balance with nature. They understood the integration of mental, spiritual, and physical health in a way just now being discovered by Western medicine.

Captain James Cook, the
first westerner credited
with discovering the
Islands

But no society is problem free, and Hawaiian society was no exception. For one thing, class lines were pronounced and uncrossable. You could never *become* a descendant of the gods; either you were born that way or you weren't. The aliʻi got the best of everything and shaped Hawaiian life in every way; in many ways, the common people didn't have power to make decisions. And women, even of the ruling class, were at a great disadvantage. They weren't allowed to eat at the same tables or from the same bowls as men. There were many foods they were denied; in fact, a woman would be killed if she were caught eating a banana or certain kinds of fish. Yet even within this system, some aliʻi women were able to gain tremendous political power.

While the Islands had a growing population, the death rate was high. Although there were some native diseases, other threats claimed more lives. Famine killed women and children; the war that raged between reigning chiefs killed many young men. In fact, the Islands were still a string of warring territories when the British finally happened upon the Islands at the very late date of 1778.* The ships of English captain James Cook stopped just briefly during a trade voyage and then continued on their way.

For the Hawaiians, life changed completely and irreversibly on January 17, 1779, when Cook's ships returned to the Islands. This time they found a suitable harbor and dropped anchor at Kealakekua on the Big Island of Hawai'i for an extended stay. The coming of Westerners set several important chains of events in motion.

First, the individual rule of islands was abolished. Kamehameha, a tall, charismatic ali'i warrior from the Big Island of Hawai'i, proved to be a brilliant strategist. He used Western guns and advisors to help defeat or intimidate the other chiefs and become the first ruler of a united island kingdom.

Second, and much less fortuitously, the sailors brought new diseases to a people with no natural immunity to them. When Cook landed, the Hawaiian population was several hundred thousand strong. Early estimates set the figure at around 300,000; more recent estimates suggest the figure may have been as high as 800,000. Sixty years later, only 70,000 natives remained. By the census of 1900, there were 30,000 full-blooded Hawaiians in Hawai'i. Measles, venereal diseases, smallpox, and even Hansen's disease (leprosy) had become facts of life.

The impact of Cook's discovery on the outside world was also far-reaching. Because the islands were perfectly positioned for commercial shipping, every powerful European country soon had a presence there.

---

*Legend had it that the Spaniards had landed earlier but if so, their arrival made no lasting impression on either the Hawaiians or the outside world.

By 1797, there were many foreigners living on the island of O'ahu, but they were mostly "deserters, vagrants, and loafers" — in other words, sailors who found they liked port better than work.

Within thirty years, however, Honolulu had become a major port. In addition to supplying provisions for incoming ships, it serviced the whaling industry and also did a brisk business in exporting sandalwood until the forests were depleted around 1830. Western merchants, professional men, and diplomats soon arrived. Not far behind were delegations of missionaries, both Protestant and Catholic. They found a native population that had recently experienced a religious and political rebellion (a movement led by an ali'i woman fed up with the *kapu* against women). They were willing to hear about the "God in a Little Black Box," as the natives called the Christian Bible.

The missionaries were scandalized by what they saw as the natives' ignorance (meaning they had no written language or schools) and their partial nudity (they lived in a tropical climate and had very different standards of decency!). Not surprisingly, the Hawaiians also had very conflicted feelings about the foreigners. The missionaries insisted they wear long clothes, desert all but one spouse (which the highest ali'i, who often had several, found cruel), and give up rum, the joys of which the sailors had just recently introduced.

Along with the new religion, Hawaiians struggled to understand two thousand years of Western thought and civilization almost overnight and to somehow meld that with centuries of Hawaiian culture. Would they be able to do so in time to retain political and cultural control of their own land and destiny? That was a critical question from the day the Westerners arrived.

In 1837, David Malo, an educated Hawaiian involved in politics, wrote to Kuhina Nui Kinau, the most powerful woman in the kingdom: "The ships of the white man have come, and smart people

King Kamehameha the
Great, wearing the royal
cloak of mamo feathers

have arrived from the great countries which you have never seen
before, they know our people are few in number and living in a
small country; they will eat us up."

His words were more prophetic than he could have known.

* * *

KAMEHAMEHA THE GREAT, the king who united the islands, had
many wives and many children. Two sons and two grandsons

reigned after him, eventually patterning their government after the British system of a constitutional monarchy.* But, since disease and infertility affected the kings the same way it did the general population, a royal line was not always easy to produce. Kamehameha IV, the last king to have a child, lost his only son at the age of four to spinal meningitis.

When Kamehameha IV died, the Legislature approved the naming of his older brother, Lot Kamehameha, to become Kamehameha V. When the latter died in 1873 without naming an heir, it became the task of the Legislature to elect the next monarch. They chose between the two highest ali'i interested in succeeding. One was William Lunalilo, a Kamehameha cousin. The other was David Kalākaua, a descendant of Kameeiamoku, a cousin of Kamehameha the Great. Lunalilo won the election, but he lived only a year and died without naming an heir.

On February 12, 1874, a second election was held. This time, Emma, the highborn widow of Kamehameha IV, ran against High Chief David Kalākaua. After a bitter contest, Kalākaua was voted king.

One of King Kalākaua's first official acts was to name his younger brother William heir apparent. The Kalākaua dynasty had begun.

*   *   *

DAVID KALĀKAUA WAS a colorful, fascinating person. A shrewd politician, he had served in the House of Nobles as well as in the courts of previous kings.

---

*This included a two-chamber legislature — much like the U.S. Congress — made up of an appointed House of Nobles and an elected House of Commons. The ruler also had an appointed cabinet of advisors; the top advisor was the premier.

While it was true that King Kalākaua was a modern constitutional monarch, it was equally true that he remained a high aliʻi. The qualities looked for in these two positions often overlapped — to be able to make executive decisions, to rule in the best interests of the people, and to be well educated and adroit in the political arena. However, some of the qualities accepted in high aliʻi — who were, after all, considered divine and unchallengeable — included an enjoyment of wine, women, and song. Kalākaua would be known to history as the Merrie Monarch.

Needless to say, the leading Western businessmen, many the sons and grandsons of the original missionaries, had been brought up to view the king's pleasures differently. Even though their relationship with the monarch was first and foremost an economic one, they didn't always approve of his personal habits and native interests. Kalākaua knew this, and he did his best to walk the line between keeping the nation's economy healthy and leading a resurgence of Hawaiian culture. (His campaign slogan had been "Hawaiʻi for the Hawaiians," and he strongly urged the native people to bear children to re-establish the native population. During his reign, the hula, the Hawaiian story-dance, was celebrated in public for the first time since the missionaries had outlawed it.) From the beginning, the balance of native and Western power was a tense one.

To Kalākaua's credit, he had a far-reaching vision of Hawaiʻi's future and its place in the world. He was interested in preserving his people's heritage as well as in using modern inventions and the tools of modern economics and education to improve the quality of his subjects' lives.

*   *   *

Queen Kapiʻolani,
Kalākaua's wife, in
royal attire

KALĀKAUA WAS ONE of ten children born to High Chiefs
Kapaakea and Keohokalole. By the time he assumed the throne,
only four of the ten were still alive. They became known as The
Four Sacred Ones of Hawaiʻi. They were David Kalākaua and his
younger brother, William Pitt Leleiohoku, and two sisters, Lydia
Liliʻuokalani and Miriam Likelike. Sadly, Kalākaua's heir, William, would die unmarried and childless just three years after his
brother's ascension.

Kalākaua's marriage to High Aliʻi Kapiʻolani, descendant of the kings of the island of Kauaʻi, remained childless.

The king's two sisters had both married Westerners. Lydia Liliʻuokalani, married to John Owen Dominis, would also never bear children.

Both of these couples did have *hānai,* or adopted children. It was customary among Hawaiians to adopt children of friends and relatives. This practice was also followed by royalty: the highest chiefs gave their children to other aliʻi to raise. This ensured close ties between ruling families. In hānai tradition, Kalākaua and Kapiʻolani raised Kapiʻolani's two nephews; Lydia Liliʻuokalani also had hānai children and grandchildren who comforted her in her old age.

However, for purposes of constitutional succession, biological children were of great importance. The Four Sacred Ones of Hawaiʻi had none.

Until October 16, 1875.

* * *

ON THAT DAY, in the bedroom of a spacious house on Emma Street in downtown Honolulu, young, vivacious Princess Miriam Likelike presented her Scottish-born husband, Archibald Cleghorn, with a daughter. The child was named Victoria Kawēkiu Lunalilo Kalaninuiahilapalapa Kaʻiulani Cleghorn. She was called Kaʻiulani.

At her birth, the king commanded the heavy guns to fire in salute. At four o'clock that afternoon, all the bells in the city began to ring joyously and continued to ring for several hours.

The Kalākaua dynasty had an heir at last. The Hawaiians had a new high aliʻi. And the two worlds that had collided a century

Princess Ka'iulani as a
toddler. Her Scots-Hawaiian
heritage made her a
born beauty.

ago had finally come to co-exist in the person of a royal baby girl.
She was the first direct heir to the throne to be part Hawaiian and
part Western.

As such, she would stand at the crossroads of history.

*   *   *

KA'IULANI WAS CHRISTENED into the Christian faith on Christmas Day of 1875. The Anglican bishop of Honolulu performed the
ceremony at St. Andrew's Cathedral, which sits just two blocks from
the palace. The baby's godparents were King Kalākaua and Queen

Kapiʻolani and the massive (and massively important) Princess Ruth, one of the last of the Kamehamehas. Kaʻiulani was awake and seemingly interested in the proceedings; everyone remarked on the fact that she didn't cry during the service.

Afterward, a grand reception was held at the old palace (the new palace was not yet built), where for the first time the two-month-old princess was introduced to her subjects. A bountiful feast was offered, and Captain Henri Berger, director of the Royal Hawaiian Band, serenaded the hundreds of guests with his new composition, "The Kaʻiulani March."

The celebration was a great success. From the tone and content of the next day's newspaper reports, it seemed certain that the tiny princess had already begun the relationship of love and mutual enchantment she would share for the rest of her life with her subjects of every race and class.

Of all Kaʻiulani's christening gifts, perhaps the most appreciated was the land in Waikīkī deeded to her by Princess Ruth. Many of the aliʻi had established homes there by the ocean so they could escape the bustle and heat of Honolulu, less than an hour away. By the time Kaʻiulani was three, the Cleghorns had moved permanently to the estate they had built on the land, which Likelike had named ʻĀinahau, or "the cool place," because of the refreshing winds that came down from the Manoa Valley.

One of Archie Cleghorn's passions was horticulture, and he turned ʻĀinahau into a garden rivaling Eden. Beyond the *kapu* sticks at the gate, which signified divine royalty, the entrance road to ʻĀinahau was bordered by towering date palms. Date and Washington palms covered the estate, and Archie added fragrant mango and teak trees, dramatic Monterey cypress, cinnamon and croton trees, and many others. He planted a wide range of exotic flowers so that there would be blossoms year round. His choices included fourteen varieties of hibiscus, Likelike's favorite white gardenias, and the flower that would become Ka'iulani's signature, Chinese jasmine. The huge tree in front of the main house, known as "Ka'iulani's banyan," was thought to be the progenitor of all the banyans in Honolulu.

'Āinahau was a little girl's paradise. There were hidden glades and footbridges over fishponds where huge tortoises basked in the sun. Brilliant peafowl strutted proudly over the grounds; Ka'iulani enjoyed them so much that to this day, the Hawaiians call Chinese jasmine "pīkake" (the Hawaiian word for "peacock") in homage to the princess's two loves.

But if Ka'iulani truly *loved* anything nonhuman at 'Āinahau, it was her snow-white riding pony, Fairy. By age seven she was an accomplished equestrian. She was often seen riding, accompanied by a groom, to visit Diamond Head Charlie at the lookout (from which he alerted O'ahu of arriving ships), or into town, where she would visit "Uncle John" Cummins, one of Honolulu's leading citizens, who she was certain had the best cows on the island.

"Uncle John," she'd announce from her horse, "I want some milk."

And the revered gentleman would excuse himself from whatever important meeting he was in and fetch her some milk himself.

*   *   *

KA'IULANI'S HERITAGE MADE her a striking young girl. She had the large dark eyes and jet-black hair of the Hawaiians coupled with the delicate facial features of the Scots. Her skin was a light tan. From both her parents she had inherited intelligence, grace, and wit — and an iron will and a flashing temper as well.

In many ways, her childhood was idyllic. But families as powerful and colorful as that into which Kaʻiulani was born seldom specialize in tranquility. As an older child, she would become aware of the political enemies lurking outside her family.

But even as a very young child, she was certainly aware of the challenges present within.

Princess Kaʻiulani as a young girl — already strong-willed like her mother

TWO

At Home with the Cleghorns

The marriage of Kaʻiulani's parents was tempestuous. Given their backgrounds and personalities, it could hardly have been otherwise.

Archibald Cleghorn had been born in Edinburgh in November of 1835, but his parents left Scotland soon after his birth to join family in New Zealand. Archie's love for horticulture was something passed on by his father, Thomas. In 1851, Thomas brought his young family to Hawaiʻi, hoping to be hired by the kingdom as a scientific gardener who would introduce new plants to the islands. Although Thomas wasn't given a position, he stayed on, opening a mercantile store on Oʻahu. When he died two years later after suffering a heart attack, his widow returned to New Zealand — but his teenaged son stayed and took over the store.

Archie Cleghorn had a head for business. He was able to expand and open stores on three other Hawaiian islands. He became a prominent businessman and was able to purchase a nice house. With Lapeka, the woman who ran his household, he had three

Kaʻiulani's parents:
Archibald Scott Cleghorn
and Princess Miriam
Likelike

daughters — Rosie, Helen, and Annie. This arrangement was not uncommon among Western men living in the islands. The girls were Cleghorns; their mother was not.

Archie enjoyed moving in court circles, being friends with King Kamehameha V and other important people. His life was nicely prescribed when, in 1868, the seventeen-year-old sister of David Kalākaua and Lydia Liliʻuokalani moved from the Big Island of Hawaiʻi to join Honolulu society. Likelike was pretty and vivacious, a talented musician and an accomplished flirt. Though already engaged to a suitable aliʻi, she was young and ready to break a few hearts before settling down. Archie, who at thirty-three was nearly twice her age, was smitten. He pursued the Hawaiian chiefess tenaciously, with all his powers of persuasion. In his favor was that her older sister, the undeniably proper Lydia, had married a Britisher. It took Archie two years to persuade Likelike to accept his proposal.

Finally, on September 22, 1870, the 35-year-old Scottish businessman and the 19-year-old Hawaiian ali'i were married at Washington Place, the home of Lydia and John Dominis.

Neither marriage ran smoothly. Archie Cleghorn and John Dominis were both wealthy Victorian gentlemen who expected to be lords of their castles, their servants, their children, and their wives. In this last category, both were in for a surprise. High ali'i — male or female — were not raised to be ruled by anyone. Archie could be blustery and demanding, but Likelike knew how to handle him. She would let him bluster, then she'd return to the Big Island and refuse to come back. Then he would send her blustery letters.

"Stop spending money! Come home at once!" he'd write. "People are talking."

In response, Likelike would goad him. She hadn't lost her knack for flirtation. "Don't listen to rumors of my misbehaving," she'd write coquettishly. "I cannot do a single thing but what the natives misconstrue my actions."

"What do you mean, *misbehaving?*" he'd roar back on paper. "Come home at once! Don't let Mary Ann persuade you to take wine — people are talking."

In 1875, Archie told his wife she couldn't go to the Big Island; she went. He told her she couldn't spend the money to build a vacation house on her property at Kaawaloa; she built one. He told her he only allowed it because at the time she was "in the family way," expecting Ka'iulani.

So Likelike got her trips, got her house, got her way. But there were some things even she couldn't control. In June of 1877, less than two years after Kaʻiulani's birth, Likelike had a miscarriage while on a ship en route to San Francisco. She would never conceive another child. From that time on, Kaʻiulani — and the future of the Hawaiian kingdom she would one day rule — became the focus of her parents' lives.

Kaʻiulani became Likelike's apt pupil in many ways. Kaʻiulani was only five when she first resisted a parental request. She was on the Big Island, visiting the Parkers (a prominent Hawaiian family whose vast ranch covered thousands of acres), and she refused to end her visit. Not surprisingly, she got her first blustery letter from Archie: "I am quite vexed. . . . If you do not come at once, I will be quite angry." He ended by saying, "I am not very well, you should have been here with me, nothing should have kept you. . . . your loving father."

One thing Kaʻiulani learned was that the pupil seldom surpasses the teacher. In an early thank-you note to Princess Ruth, she wrote: "Dear Mama Nui: Thank you for the nice hat you sent me. It fits so nicely Mama wanted it, but I would not let her have it. Thank you for the corn and watermelons, they do taste so good. Are you well? With much love from your little girl, Kaʻiulani. P.S. I want you to give Miss Barnes [her governess] a native name."

Not surprisingly, another note was soon to follow: "Dear Mama Nui: I want another hat. Mama Likelike has taken the hat you sent me. Are you better now. When are you coming home. With much love. From your little girl — Kaʻiulani."

*   *   *

AS WILLFUL AND mercurial as she was, Likelike was known as magnanimous and generous to everyone she loved. Although she could be imperious and quick-tempered — she once smacked a

"Mama Nui," Ka'iulani's godmother. Formally known as Princess Ruth Keelikolani, she was the half-sister of kings Kamehameha IV and V.

groom with a whip for not keeping the carriage properly polished — she was known as the consummate hostess in the islands, entertaining both island society and international visitors with proper decorum and a natural flair. She also served as governor of the island of Hawai'i from 1878 to 1880 and always thought of the Big Island as her true home.

Still, Likelike's fights with Archie continued. In August of 1883, Likelike wrote her strongest letter yet to her husband from her retreat on the Big Island: "You always blame me in everything and I am getting tired of it. I will have to kill myself then you won't have me to growl at all the time. I think we are better separated . . . as you

Kaʻiulani (between the two kāhili bearers) enjoys a lūʻau
with her childhood friends at ʻĀinahau.

don't love me and I don't love you, so I will simply say, 'God bless the good.'"

Was Likelike serious about her suicidal threat? Given her volatile personality, it is tempting to write it off as more high drama, another sign of her controlling personality. However, given the full story of her life, this letter does raise troubling questions about her state of mind.

Yet, as dramatic as her threats were, Likelike came back.

While Kaʻiulani learned to copy her mother's imperiousness, she also learned at a young age to temper it with kindness.

Elsie Jaeger, a childhood playmate of Kaʻiulani's, later told the story of the day a number of friends were playing under the banyan tree at ʻĀinahau. Kaʻiulani, pretending to be the old-style Queen of All Hawaiʻi, commanded them all to fall prostrate before her. Elsie, of high aliʻi blood herself, refused to do so. The two girls raged at each other, and Elsie punctuated her diatribe by hurling a stick in the direction of the princess. To her horror, it struck Kaʻiulani in the face and caused a cut above one eye. Elsie was immediately contrite. After all, Kaʻiulani was *kapu*, sacred, and no one was allowed to even touch her without permission — let alone hit her with a stick! Yet the two friends quickly made up, and all was forgotten until the children were inside eating.

"Kaʻiulani, what has happened to your forehead?" Likelike asked.

Elsie, terrified of the displeasure of the mercurial older princess, imagined a swift and painful end to her short life until Kaʻiulani said with a twinkle, "Nothing, Mama. I fell down."

* * *

IT'S SAFE TO assume that few emotions went unexpressed in the Cleghorn family and that volatile behavior was fairly common. Yet in many ways Kaʻiulani had a secure and well-ordered childhood — in large part due to the influence of two long-term governesses. The first was Miriam Barnes, a stalwart woman who was completely devoted to the young princess, whom she had raised from a toddler. A devout Christian, she was well-liked by the family, and had a sense of her own mission strong enough to withstand royal rages if it meant seeing to the best interests of young Kaʻiulani. In fact, when she and the princess visited the Big Island, she wrote many notes to ʻĀinahau informing Archie and Likelike what was best for their daughter. Miss Barnes nursed Kaʻiulani through illnesses, was her constant traveling companion, and did much to teach the willful little girl the manners and restraint expected in polite society.

King Kalākaua's coronation in February of 1883 was a proud event for both the governess and her young charge. Sadly, Kaʻiulani's

The interior of the main house at 'Āinahau

godmother, Princess Ruth, died that spring — and beloved Miss Barnes died unexpectedly that summer.

For nearly two years, a succession of governesses were tried and found wanting.

Then, in the spring of 1885, Mrs. Wallace, the wife of the Anglican bishop, suggested a young teacher from a parish school in New York state. Gertrude Gardinier agreed to come for a trial period.

When she arrived on May 8, 1885, it was as if a new sun rose in the life of the nine-year-old princess. Miss Gardinier was not only extraordinarily beautiful; she was spirited and had both great imagination and great common sense. Ka'iulani was immediately smitten.

The day of her arrival, Ka'iulani showed Miss Gardinier the

main house, which was charmingly decorated in the style known as "Victorian clutter." Tables, chairs, and loveseats filled the main room; paintings and photographs covered the walls. Five steps led up to the family's living quarters, which included bedrooms for Kaʻiulani and her governess, with a shared sitting room in between. The lānai surrounding the house was broad and well-used; in fact, this was where meals were most often eaten.

Miss Gardinier had planned to spend several weeks visiting with the Wallaces, but Likelike had other plans. The governess moved in to ʻĀinahau almost right away. She wrote home describing her new employers. Archie impressed her as "a man of dignified presence, a genial host, devoted to his family and home, and always a most courteous gentleman." She described Princess Likelike as "small, graceful and stylish with pretty dimpled arms and hands. She has an imperious and impulsive nature and is considered quite haughty by some, but she is very genial in her home and is always most thoughtful and considerate of those she likes." And of Kaʻiulani herself, the new governess reported, "She is the fragile, *spirituelle* type, but very vivacious, with beautiful large, expressive dark eyes. She proves affectionate, high-spirited, at times quite willful, though usually reasonable and very impulsive and generous."

The two soon became inseparable companions. Kaʻiulani was fascinated by Miss Gardinier's clothing and the photographs that she'd brought of her family back in New York. Immediately she sent gifts to her governess's mother and brother, accompanied by this letter:

Dear Mrs. Gardinier: I thought I would write you a letter. Miss Gardinier and I went to Honolulu this morning. It has been raining today, but it is clearing up now. I had a nice sea bath today. Miss Gardinier would not venture in this morning. I am going to study very hard and try to learn my lessons well, and then hope to

Kaʻiulani with Miss
Gardinier, her beloved
governess

come to the States some day and visit you. I will send you my picture when I have some taken. Miss Gardinier and I are going to
ride horseback some day when she learns to. I have a pretty little
pony of my own and I am not afraid to ride it. My pony is only
four years old, and I am nine years old. Goodbye, from Kaʻiulani
Cleghorn.

For the first two weeks, lessons were suspended so that the two
could get to know each other. Miss Gardinier bravely took up horseback riding and accompanied Kaʻiulani to see Diamond Head
Charlie at his lookout.

Queen Emma, King
Kalākaua's rival

But this happy time was marred by a tragic event, one that some said was the result of *anaana* — a powerful priest praying someone to death. In fact, soon after Miss Gardinier's arrival, the rumor circulated through the Islands, and it's likely that Ka'iulani heard it through the servants' chatter, if not through the discussions of her own parents.

The rumor was about King Kalākaua and his rival for the throne, Queen Emma. Although the two came to a public truce soon after Kalākaua's election, it seems certain that some private enmity remained between them. In a letter to a friend, Emma (though an avid Anglican) described how a kahuna had instructed her to "take a young lamb to be eaten at noon, with three drops of its heart blood and three drops of gall mixed in a glass of brandy, which I am to drink before eating. The blood is the hearts' blood of our people and the gall is the gall of these times. As a sign on that day, the heavens will be cloudless. And Kalākaua's birth tree, with all its roots and branches, will be cut off."

Queen Emma died on April 25, 1885. Although she had suffered ill health for a while prior to her death, the rumor was that she had been prayed to death by a powerful kahuna — some claimed by Kalākaua himself. It was Hawaiian custom that when a high aliʻi died, all aliʻi of high rank gathered together for a mourning period of three weeks. Likelike and Aunt Lydia were among those who mourned Emma.

Miss Gardinier arrived in Hawaiʻi on May 8; Queen Emma's funeral was held on May 14 at Kawaiahaʻo Church. (Although Emma was Anglican and had worshiped at St. Andrews, this Congregational church was much larger than the Anglican church; for the simple reason of seating capacity it was the church of choice for state funerals.)

King Kalākaua did something unexpected: he attended Queen Emma's funeral in the company of his young niece, Kaʻiulani. While this act was of symbolic importance, affirming Kaʻiulani's place in the future of the dynasty, the proceedings frightened the girl. When she returned home (and without Miss Gardinier's help, either with her feelings or with her spelling), Kaʻiulani wrote to Queen Kapiʻolani:

My Dear Auntie: Papa Moi [her name for Kalākaua, which means "papa king"] and I have just come from the frunral of the old queen. We did not see you there after the parade. Papa says I must write and thank you for the flowers you gave me and the nice little ring.

I do not like frunrals they are sad, and all the noise that the kanakers make scares me something bad. Aunty will you and the Moi Alii come and see me some time soon?

I must play just a bit more and then my govruness makes me take my afternoon rest, so that I will grow big and strong and be a good girl.

Love to you and the King from
Ka'iulani

Fortunately, such traumatic events were rare. And this event, although it troubled Ka'iulani, was soon overshadowed by her deepening relationship with Miss Gardinier, who worked hard to provide Ka'iulani with an education befitting a future queen.

Miss Gardinier purposefully became acquainted with island society and court circles. She tutored her pupil not only in academic subjects but also in protocol. Morning lessons focused on music, reading, writing, and history; afternoon lessons included attending social functions and teaching Ka'iulani to carry out the duties expected of a princess.

The little girl very much needed someone she could look to for direction and guidance. An incident during the first week's lessons showed that Miss Gardinier was up to the task. It was a small thing: Ka'iulani's spelling book fell to the floor. She made no move to pick it up, explaining to the puzzled governess, "I cannot pick it up, Miss Gardinier. You see, I am a princess. And princesses cannot stoop."

The delicate balance of power was at stake when Miss Gardinier answered, "Very well, Ka'iulani. But, as your governess, I cannot pick it up for you."

The pupil accepted the implied countering power of this response. The answer to her problem was simple: she rang the small

A view of Diamond Head, where Ka'iulani frequently went riding

bell that sat on her desk, and her faithful retainer Kanoah darted in, picked up the book, and returned it to her young mistress. The lesson continued.

Ka'iulani's favorite day of the week was Sunday. In her journal Miss Gardinier described the order of the day's events. She and Ka'iulani would rise early, have a glass of warm milk, and take a morning ride, usually to see Diamond Head Charlie, who would have coffee and rock-hard sea biscuits ready for them. Then they'd canter back along the beach, stopping if they wanted to gather shells, which the attendants riding with them would happily carry home.

After breakfast on the lānai, the family would go to services at St. Andrews. Sometimes they stayed in town to lunch at Washington Place, the stately home of Uncle John and Aunt Lydia, which was actually owned — and run — by Uncle John's widowed mother. More often they had Sunday dinner at home at two o'clock. After that, the family relaxed, taking afternoon siestas under the welcoming shade of the large banyan.

After their rest, Kaʻiulani and Miss Gardinier studied the Bible and the Anglican catechism. Kaʻiulani was very interested in both. Miss Gardinier was very pleased by the young princess's knowledge of the Bible and her grasp of theological subjects. In fact, even at this young age, Kaʻiulani's faith and her relationship to God were extremely important to her. This was a vital relationship that she would have all her life. She would question God — and the actions of her fellow Christians — often during her lifetime. But Christianity became a guiding light that would take her through very difficult times.

In fact, a dry religion "on paper" would have done the princess very little good. She had been taught, as had many islanders, that there are primal, powerful forces at work in the spirit world. She needed to understand the Christian God as powerful and loving to counter stories of the "dark side" of Huna — which had so recently seemed evident in Queen Emma's death.

On Sundays after Bible study, the fun would begin. By late afternoon, guests would begin to arrive at ʻĀinahau. Mama's family was especially talented at music. Before William's death, each of the four "Sacred Ones" had his or her own glee club for which they composed music. Uncle William's group had been all men, but Likelike's and Lydia's were both choruses of mixed voices, men and women. Kalākaua himself had written "Hawaiʻi Ponoʻī," the national anthem. Likelike was also a very prolific composer. But Lydia always seemed to win the friendly competition. Several of her songs became well known, including "Aloha ʻOe."

Joining the Cleghorns on these Sunday afternoons were musicians, friends, and other family members. Kaʻiulani was always especially happy when her cousins by marriage (they were the sons of

Members of Ka'iulani's family (ca. 1880). The group includes Princess Lili'oukalani
and Princess Likelike (seated, middle), and Thomas Cleghorn, John Dominis,
and Archie Cleghorn (standing).

Queen Kapi'olani's sister), "The Three Princes," were home from
military school in California and could join in the festivities.

To a young girl of nine, the Piikoi boys seemed tremendously
worldly and mature. David Kawānanakoa, called Koa, was seven years
her senior. Handsome and confident, he was the favored oldest son. Although the age difference seemed extreme in her youth, it was Koa with
whom Ka'iulani would have the longest-lasting, most complex relationship. Rumors of romantic entanglement and of unrequited feelings
on one side or the other would follow them throughout their lives.

The middle prince, Edward Abel Keliiahoui, was in a difficult position. A year younger than Koa, he was physically smaller than either
of his brothers. He also had a weaker constitution and fought illness

"The Three Princes" — Kūhiō, Koa (seated), and Edward — wearing their school uniforms

more frequently. He had been "hanai"ed to Kapiʻolani's younger sister, so he was not thought of as a foster son of the king and queen.

At thirteen, Jonah Kūhiō Kalanianaʻole was closest to Kaʻiulani's age. Kūhiō, nicknamed "Cupid" by a French teacher because of his deceptively "angelic" dimples, was athletic, rambunctious, and lots of fun. He excelled at surfing, rowing, and the Hawaiian game of *pio,* a kind of tag. If he thought someone was being treated unfairly, he didn't hesitate to leap to their defense; if anything, he got into scrapes and fights more often than his teachers thought he should. But he had a fine sense of humor and was quick to forgive. His mischievous nature guaranteed that the nickname "Cupid" would follow him well into his teens.

Kaʻiulani loved those Sunday evenings, with a bountiful

spread of Hawaiian food, good friends gathered around, her three handsome cousins laughing in the gardens, her parents' arguments forgotten, and Miss Gardinier at her side. As the inevitable croquet game ended, kukui-nut torches were lit against the night, and to the accompaniment of the ocean waves and the gentle swaying of the palms, the singing began. Men's and women's voices wove their spell, surrounding royalty, guests, and retainers alike. And the joy of island life bound them together, cares forgotten.

* * *

DESPITE GOOD TIMES like these, Kaʻiulani didn't seem to have her usual energy that summer. By the end of the summer, Miss Gardinier was concerned enough about Kaʻiulani's "listlessness" to bring it up to her mother. Likelike thought a change of scene would help; not surprisingly, she decided they should go to Kaawaloa, their vacation home on the Big Island.

This excursion was a wonderful restorative. The Big Island of Hawaiʻi was much less Westernized than the bustling capital of Oʻahu. Heavy gowns of silks and satins were immediately shed for light *holokū*; social calls were made not in tortoise-shell carriages but on donkeys. Away from protocol and achingly polite society, Kaʻiulani suddenly felt released from the cares of the world. She could jump and swim in the freshwater pond on the property, and watch the funny-looking, brilliantly colored fish of Kealekekua Bay just outside her door. She loved studying the sweeping, primal *pali* (cliffs) that rose above the bay; so many rainbows had appeared above them that the bay had been named "pathway of the gods." Legend said that Lono, the happy, mischievous Hawaiian god of the harvest, slid down those rainbows, much as children slide down a banister.

Lessons were suspended for the holiday, so Miss Gardinier was free to be Kaʻiulani's friend and protectress. They had male retainers, of course, but generally their retreat at Kaawaloa was a woman's world, where kings and papas and politics seldom intruded.

On the morning of October 16, Kaʻiulani woke early, with a mounting excitement even stronger than she felt on Christmas. Eagerly she awoke Kanoah and put on the new dress that hung waiting. Her hair brushed and bowed, she ran to prod Miss Gardinier to breakfast.

"Why, Kaʻiulani, what's your hurry?" her governess asked with a twinkle.

But everyone knew how special this day was — it was the princess's tenth birthday.

In honor of the occasion, Mama had planned a grand lūʻau. Her invitation had been so widely accepted that a new, broader lānai had been added to the house in anticipation.

Sure enough, no sooner had dawn brought the first rays of sun over the palis than long lines of well-wishers appeared, traveling down the steep paths to greet their princess. Aliʻi, kanaka, Westerners — they all came with love, bearing gifts and flowers for Kaʻiulani. The girl stood tall on the lānai, her heart filled with *aloha* as young mothers with barefoot children, wizened grandmas and grandpas, fisherfolk and wealthy ranchers bowed before her, kissed her hand, and presented gifts.

Kaʻiulani knew she would never forget this day. As in times past, her people owed her loyalty and devotion as their aliʻi. And she, in return, owed them a happy and healthy life in their land.

The next day she would return to Oʻahu and to an official birthday celebration attended by the king and queen. But no trappings of royalty taught her as much about why she must reign with a heart for the people as that day at Kaawaloa, when she received the unstinting aloha of her people and returned it with all her heart.

Princess Ka'iulani, showing grace and royal poise at a young age

THREE

So Hard to Say Good-bye

Kaʻiulani's favorite tenth-birthday gift was her own flag, sewn for her by some women from Honolulu. It was a red silk banner featuring the coat of arms of the Kalākaua dynasty, with the addition of a cross embroidered on a white background in the middle. In many ways the symbolism was appropriate.

As time passed, politics intruded more and more upon Cleghorn family life. Archie Cleghorn had long been a member of the House of Nobles. When Kalākaua became king, he quickly appointed his brother-in-law a member of the Privy Council, the king's closest advisors. When Archie and other legislators and statesmen held spirited discussions at ʻĀinahau, all the children were shooed from the room — except Kaʻiulani. It was understood from the beginning that she was involved in matters of state.

What she heard as 1886 began was often troubling. Archie, while devoted to the future of the island monarchy, was often critical of the king. Early in their marriage, he wrote to Likelike that Kalākaua was "neither feared nor loved." This was more likely the sentiment among Westerners than among the native population. (During Kalākaua's reign, there were two main political parties. The Royalists were dedicated to the monarchy and Hawaiian self-rule. The Reformers were largely representing Western business interests.)

Kalākaua had a weakness for grand visions of the future — and the schemers who claimed they could bring them about. One such "visionary" who had charmed him was a man named Caesar Moreno, an Italian with a checkered past who brought the king dreams of transatlantic cables, trade routes with China, and great wealth for Hawai'i (and the king himself). Honolulu's business community had been alarmed when the king made Moreno his premier (the top advisor of the Privy Council) and dismissed his current council members to name men of Moreno's choosing.

Kalākaua was finally forced to sever ties with Moreno, who had so angered the business community that he was lucky to escape the islands with his life.

Kalākaua's current premier was not much better liked by the Westerners. Although Ka'iulani felt the gray-bearded Walter Murray Gibson was a kind man with a heart for Hawaiians, others were not so generous in their assessment. He certainly had a "creative" past, which included becoming the leader of the Mormon colony on the island of Lana'i while using his flock's funds to buy the land in his own name. He was sure that he and Kalākaua could find great personal wealth while turning Hawai'i into a world power.

One thing was certain. The gulf between Westerners and Hawaiians was growing wider — and the *haole* (white people) were making increasingly loud and insistent criticisms of the king.

Ka'iulani learned early that in politics people are always angry with each other. So she listened to the Hawaiian legislators and the ambassadors from other nations as they talked in her parlor, trying

Hawaiians near Honolulu Beach enjoying one of Kaʻiulani's favorite pastimes — surfing.

to learn from their heated discussions. But for a ten-year-old, personal crises often seemed more real than those in the palace and Aliʻi Hale, where the legislators met.

One such crisis occurred that summer.

Kaʻiulani loved the ocean. She was an expert surfer, and was known for going out farther along the reefs than most were willing to venture. She didn't get to surf every day, but she was allowed a daily swim, what she called a "sea bath," that she always enjoyed.

One day, Miss Gardinier called to her to come out of her "bath" and get dressed. But Kaʻiulani didn't want to come. She disregarded her governess's entreaties for as long as possible.

Finally she walked reluctantly onto the beach, letting her waiting maids dress her. But she was tired of trying so hard to be a "proper young lady." With eyes flashing, she pulled away and ran back into the waves, not caring that her fancy dress got soaked through.

Miss Gardinier cared. In exasperation, the governess ran into the water, grasped Kaʻiulani by the shoulders, and lightly slapped her face.

It's hard to imagine the impact of that slap. Kaʻiulani was kapu, sacred, and she was never even touched except by a favored few. No one had ever laid a hand on her in anger. She was shocked — and furious.

"I'll tell my mother!" she cried.

Miss Gardinier decided to speak first. She stalked to the grass shack on the property that Likelike had turned into a modern boudoir and office. She reported the incident, and Likelike was indeed gravely distressed. But not, as Miss Gardinier recorded in her journal, because of Kaʻiulani's disobedience. Barely containing herself, Likelike explained, "You see, Miss Gardinier, Kaʻiulani is a princess. And a princess cannot be punished."

Miss Gardinier replied, "I'm very sorry, Your Highness, but a princess must learn to understand obedience, especially if it is for her own good. If she cannot be disciplined when necessary, then I cannot teach her. I herewith tender my resignation."

A few hours later, Kaʻiulani knocked on her governess's door with a trembling hand. She had won, but it had not been a triumph. "Miss Gardinier," she said, "I realize I was disobedient this afternoon, and I am very sorry."

Miss Gardinier replied, "Kaʻiulani, there's something you need to think about. If you, as a princess, do not obey any authority, how can you expect obedience from others?"

Close to tears, Kaʻiulani promised never to disobey her governess again. Then she flung herself into the woman's arms. "Oh, Miss Gardinier, *please* don't go away!"

Much to the little girl's relief, after continued talks with Likelike, Miss Gardinier agreed to stay on for another year. She proved herself to be exactly what the young princess needed. She was intimately concerned with the welfare of her charge, but she had a strong enough sense of self apart from the royal family that she would not hesitate to leave if she felt compromised. This gave Kaʻiulani a resource Likelike had never had: someone willing to set limits, to say no. Kaʻiulani came to depend on this strength. She hoped that each year Miss Gardinier would promise to stay on. But it was not to be.

*   *   *

KAʻIULANI'S ELEVENTH BIRTHDAY was treated as a very "grown up" occasion. Her party didn't involve children's games or the spontaneous aloha of the year before; instead, it was a political event. The guests were all the members of the legislature and their wives.

The importance of the occasion had been drilled into the girl — but she had long understood the obligations that came with being born royal. For the party, Kaʻiulani was dressed in a fashionable frock; she graciously accepted gifts and was charming to each giver. While it might not have been the party she would have planned, she did receive a certain satisfaction from knowing her role and carrying it off well.

According to the newspapers, the offered feast at ʻĀinahau was bountiful. After the sit-down luncheon, King Kalākaua stood and bowed toward his niece. "Ladies and gentlemen," he smiled, "I arise to propose the health of Her Royal Highness, Princess Kaʻiulani. On this occasion I am proud to pay this compliment to my niece as a member of the direct line. I hope that she may fill her position in the future to the credit of the nation."

This toast was answered by Royalist Sam Wilder: "May she indeed live to be the 'Hope of the Nation.' May her education be . . . such that when, in the natural events of life, she may rule over this land, it may be a rule of wisdom, always retaining the love of her people. Surely all here will say with me 'Aloha nui' to the Princess Kaʻiulani."

"In the natural events of life, she may rule over this land." Heady words for an eleven-year-old.

The king seemed very pleased with the party; both Royalists and Reformers showed the princess love and respect. Not only that, but an entire room had to be given over to the display of Kaʻiulani's presents.

For Kaʻiulani herself, the emotional high of the birthday cele-

At the tender age of eleven, the princess was already "the hope of the nation."

bration was soon brought low by traumatic news: Miss Gardinier announced that she was engaged to be married in the spring and would be leaving the Cleghorns' employ.

Kaʻiulani had come to know her governess as the rock to which she could cling, a protection against the changeable winds of her parents' tempers and the buffeting waves of national politics.

Betrayed and frightened, she did not hide her feelings about the cause of what was for her a terrible situation. First, she made a long thumbnail gash through Miss Gardinier's photograph of her intended, Albert Heydtmann. Then, when he came to call, she walked up to him and announced, "Mr. Heydtmann, I hate you."

48

The unfortunate gentleman was alarmed. "Why, Princess Ka'iulani! What have I ever done to make you say that?"

To Ka'iulani, the answer seemed obvious. "You are going to take Miss Gardinier away. She came to Hawai'i for me, not for you!"

Much to her dismay, no one seemed inclined to take her part. In fact, Likelike even offered to hold the wedding reception at 'Āinahau.

But there would be even greater highs and lows before the year played out.

*   *   *

NOVEMBER 16 WAS King Kalākaua's fiftieth birthday. The Royalists in the legislature had pushed through funding for a celebration — and what festivities there were! The island enjoyed a week-long party, including lu'aū, regattas, and a torchlight parade. It was impossible for Ka'iulani, who was among those at the center of these activities, not to imagine what it would be like when *she* was the monarch being fêted.

Once again, the gulf between Royalists and Reformers widened. One faction looked at the goodwill of the week as proving the king's popularity; the other railed against the "extravagant expenditure" while public works were being neglected.

The funds appropriated for Kalākaua's celebration were only one of the Reformers' monetary complaints. King Kalākaua and Premier Gibson had also won an appropriation for Hawai'i to establish a navy.

Yet, as Christmas approached, the importance of these things was dwarfed for Ka'iulani by the turn of events at home.

Likelike, who had always been so full of life and energy, suddenly took to her bed. She refused meals in her darkened sickroom. The doctor was summoned, but he could find nothing wrong with her except weakness from lack of nourishment.

Part of the Jubilee festivities at ʻIolani Palace,
including a procession of kāhili bearers (left)

Kaʻiulani sat with her daily, and Aunt Lydia came from Hono-lulu. Both of them tried to talk of the future, of any topic that might catch Likelike's interest. Nothing worked.

Christmas drew nearer. Its festive air and decorations of green boughs and red velvet bows provided a sad contrast to the ever more frightening atmosphere at home.

Miss Gardinier continued Kaʻiulani's daily lessons, her cheerful optimism lacing Kaʻiulani's spirits with a desperate hope. One of the things that heartened Kaʻiulani was a royal "family project" of sorts. Members of the royal family had each underwritten a new stained-glass window for St. Andrew's Cathe-dral. Likelike's window would illustrate Joseph being pulled from the pit. Ka'iulani's would illustrate the most powerful of Christian beliefs — the resurrection of Jesus Christ. As Likelike's condition continued to deteriorate, Ka'iulani clung to the hope inherent in the meaning of the resurrection.

*   *   *

AGAIN, THE RUMORS.

In the old days, when a powerful ali'i wanted to curry favor with the gods, he or she would offer a human sacrifice. The more powerful the *mana,* or spiritual power, of the sacrifice, the more powerful the help from the god.

Likelike's symptoms matched nothing the Western doctors could diagnose. As her condition worsened with no explanation, the idea that she was being prayed to death gained hold. But why? She was popular and well-loved among Hawaiians, and she was no threat to the haole.

The easiest and most sensational target was again King Kalākaua. If nothing else, the accusation gave the Westerners renewed ammunition for their claims that the king was "trafficking in idols" and practicing sorcery.

While there was absolutely no proof that Kalākaua was involved in any such practice, especially against his beloved younger sister, he certainly was in need of intervention, divine or otherwise. He and Premier Gibson had launched the first (and only) "warship" in the Hawaiian navy, sending it to Samoa to try to make a treaty with King Malietoa and begin the fledgling confederacy known as "Oceania."

The mission was an expensive fiasco. The boat was barely seaworthy. The crew, recruited from the boys' reformatory, mutinied the day before sailing. The Hawaiian ambassador was a barely functioning alcoholic. And King Malietoa's signing of the treaty brought an immediate threat of a declaration of war against Hawaiʻi from Germany, which had a strong interest in Samoa.

The visionary mission to unite the independent kingdoms of the Pacific ended in disgrace, sinking many thousands of dollars with the dreams of Oceania.

And on January 16, the active volcano of Moana Loa erupted on the Big Island, destroying property and sending residents fleeing for their lives before its molten rivers of red-hot lava.

None of this mattered to eleven-year-old Kaʻiulani. All she cared about was willing her mother off her sickbed and seeing her healthy again.

Archie was also alarmed. Usually thrifty, he arranged a trip to San Francisco for his wife and daughter that the two could take as soon as the doctors said Likelike was well enough to travel. Likelike loved visiting San Francisco. But even this gesture got no response from the ailing princess.

On February 2, Kaʻiulani was called from her morning lessons to the sickroom. Frightened by the urgency of the summons, she entered the darkened room hesitantly.

"Go, all of you," Likelike whispered to the retainers who were nursing her.

Obediently they left, closing the door with a soft thud.

With what little energy she had, Likelike summoned her daughter to the bed. Kaʻiulani felt vulnerable and afraid as she sat in the adjacent chair. The woman beside her didn't look like Mama at all. Her skin was gray in the muted light, and she was eerily thin.

"Kaʻiulani, listen to me," she said. "I am going to die very soon."

The stricken girl leaned forward to protest, but her mother held up a hand to stop her.

The broken voice coming through the parched lips was barely recognizable as she said, "I have seen your future very plainly. You

Princess Likelike in a
formal portrait

will go far away for a very long time. You will never marry. And you
will never be queen."

Ka'iulani could not take in the enormity of what she was hearing. Was her mother trying to frighten her? Or warn her?

Sobs choked her, and she fell upon the bed, crying, "Mama, no!
You can't die! You can't! Please!"

Hearing the tumult, Archie opened the bedroom door and
rushed in.

"Go now," said Princess Likelike to her daughter.

"Mama, no!" Ka'iulani repeated as she was ushered from the
room.

Ka'iulani ran to find her solace, her rock — Miss Gardinier. Weeping, she threw herself into her governess's arms and repeated her mother's pronouncements.

Trying to calm the terrified child, Miss Gardinier countered with common sense. "Very often, when people are as ill as Her Highness, they believe they see things in the future. But it's only part of their illness."

But Ka'iulani was shaken to the core. A mother's death is a profound loss for any child. But if Likelike's vision was true, Ka'iulani would lose not only her mother but also her home, her future family, and her life's purpose in one harsh blow. In fact, Ka'iulani would deal with the effects of her mother's pronouncement — spiritual, emotional, and actual — for the rest of her life.

*   *   *

THE FIRST PART of Princess Likelike's prophecy was fulfilled within the day. She died shortly after four P.M. that afternoon.

If Ka'iulani had been frightened by the wailing of the kanaka during Queen Emma's funeral procession, that February night was her most horrific nightmare come to life.

For as the news spread, hundreds of Hawaiians, men and women, young and old, began arriving at the home of their lost ali'i. Haunting death wails filled the air, practically shaking the wooden house where Princess Likelike's body was being prepared for its midnight ride.

Miss Gardinier greeted the formal callers; Archie and Ka'iulani sought refuge in their rooms.

Promptly at midnight, the slow, solemn torchlight procession began as the princess's body was taken by carriage to lie in state in the throne room at 'Iolani Palace.

Princess Likelike lying in state at 'Iolani Palace, where thousands came to mourn her

Certainly no one in Honolulu slept that night. Between the primal wails and chants of the Hawaiians and the bobbing torches of the mourners following the princess's carriage on foot, the night was wound with grief.

Ka'iulani and Archie rode in the first carriage behind the casket, followed by the king and queen, then Aunt Lydia and Uncle John. Early the next morning, there was a private Anglican service for the immediate family in the throne room where Likelike lay in a robe of white satin, surrounded by *kāhili* bearers, who waved their tall, feather-topped sticks over the body of the chiefess. On her gown were pinned the Royal Orders of Kalākaua and Kamehameha. At the foot of her bier was a Christian cross; at its head was a crimson cushion that held her coronet and other Royal Orders.

After the family service, the doors were opened, and lines of thousands of mourners began to file past the bier of the beloved princess. Ka'iulani realized in a new way that her grief, like her life, was public. Loyal subjects gathered up gardenias — Likelike's favorite flower — and brought them to 'Āinahau. When the thousands of blossoms were burned, they left a sweet, heavy scent that lingered over Waikīkī for days.

This public mourning was difficult enough. Yet for Ka'iulani, the hardest part was to follow. She was left behind, without her father or her governess, in the palace where her dead mother lay. As a high-ranking ali'i, she had to stay at the palace with the body for three weeks.

The angry volcano on the Big Island stopped spouting lava. This was a cause for rejoicing — but it also added fuel to the rumors that Likelike had been prayed to death to appease the gods. It couldn't have been easy for Ka'iulani during those three weeks, living in a palace that housed not only her mother's body but the king who was rumored to have killed her.

Yet Papa and Mama Mō'ī were also grieving. As time passed, Ka'iulani willed herself not to be affected by the accusations made against her uncle by his enemies.

Miss Gardinier sensed Ka'iulani's deep emotional needs and made daily visits from Waikīkī to the palace to comfort Ka'iulani, to walk the palace grounds with her and talk and read.

The coda to this requiem of loss was the double funeral on Sunday, February 23. The private service for 150 guests began at 9:30 in the morning in the throne room. Ka'iulani stood at the head of the casket, between her father and the king. The funeral at one in the afternoon, although also by invitation only, packed the throne room and surrounding lānais with dignitaries and friends.

After the Christian service, the coffin was taken down the palace steps to the catafalque. According to Hawaiian custom, it was pulled by men instead of horses. And so the solemn procession began, with

The burial service at the royal crypt at Nuʻuanu

guns booming every minute and thousands of weeping Hawaiians following behind. Their destination was the royal crypt at Nuʻuanu, up toward the *pali* north of Honolulu. It was a two-hour march, the same one Kaʻiulani had taken following Queen Emma's casket. At the crypt, the remainder of the Anglican burial service was read. The Hawaiian choir chanted the Twenty-Second Psalm, and a final hymn, "Now the Laborer's Task Is Over," was sung.

Finally Kaʻiulani boarded the family carriage with her father to return at long last to ʻĀinahau.

Home. But a home where Likelike's rages and loving words, her laughter and music, would be heard no more.

A home which now had an eleven-year-old mistress.

Things would never be the same.

Robert Louis Stevenson, the "unexpected friend," with King Kalākaua in Honolulu, 1889

FOUR

An Unexpected Friend

To Ka'iulani's amazement, life went on. By mid-April, the palace had officially finished its period of mourning. The king threw a grand ball (which Ka'iulani did not attend) for visiting dignitaries. Many citizens came to watch the proceedings, because for the first time, as evening fell, 'Iolani Palace was ablaze with electric lights.

Kalākaua was determined to bring electricity to his kingdom, even though much of the United States didn't have it yet. That night the festive palace, aglow with light and filled with waltzing couples, highlighted the best that Western contact had brought to the Islands.

That same month, Hawai'i sent a delegation to attend the Golden Jubilee of England's Queen Victoria. Britain had long been a valued ally of Hawai'i, and it was thought proper that Queen Kapi'olani, along with Heir Apparent Princess Lili'uokalani (Aunt Lydia) and her husband John Dominis, attend the festivities celebrating Queen Victoria's fifty years on the throne.

Kaʻiulani was named for the British ruler — Victoria was her first name — and she had always been fascinated by the life of the august woman who had become queen at such a young age. Victoria had married for love, had a large family, and had overseen the expansion of the British Empire. This made her a role model for Kaʻiulani and gave the young princess hope, especially in the wake of her mother's prophecy. Miss Gardinier fanned the flames of her interest in the trip; together they charted the royal Hawaiians' travel course on world maps. Kaʻiulani wrote to her relatives, clearly envying them. In a letter she wrote to her Aunt Lydia on June 3, she said, "From what I have read in the papers, I thought you must be having a most delightful time; how I wish that I could have been with you to see all the grand sights in those beautiful cities."

Kaʻiulani was thrilled to get missives in response detailing the trip. It seemed to be a great success, with Hawaiian aliʻi accepted as equals of the rulers of other world nations. This was especially important because Kamehameha IV had met with much prejudice in America just after the Civil War because of his dark complexion.

All of Aunt Lydia's reports of the Jubilee were glowing, as were the newspaper accounts of the honors bestowed upon the Hawaiians. Never had so many ruling monarchs and heads of governments gathered in one place as descended upon London in 1887.

However, Queen Victoria's journals, which were made public decades later, add a sobering footnote. She reported that both the King of the Belgians and the King of Saxony refused to accompany Princess Liliʻuokalani to the Jubilee Supper because she was "colored." This created a behind-the-scenes furor until Queen Victoria herself commanded her son Albert to accompany Aunt Lydia.

Kaʻiulani, safe in the "garden" of her islands, knew nothing of prejudice except that which she saw expressed between rival factions in her own kingdom.

Princess Liliʻuokalani and Queen Kapiʻolani (seated) in England in 1887,
during the Golden Jubilee

Her father Archie had been given positions of increasing importance in the Kalākaua government. In the absence of Uncle John Dominis, he was called on to act as governor of Oʻahu. This was not a casual appointment — it may have been part of the king's larger plan. Some suspected that the king had purposely sent his wife and sister away because he had another get-rich-quick scheme. In any case, in June the king was personally linked to a financial swindle along with Premier Gibson, and anti-Gibson feeling flared in the business community.

Whether the charges of the swindle were totally fabricated (as the Royalists charged) or true (as the Reformers insisted), this was the rallying point that the Hawaiian League needed. The league had been formed early in 1887 by haole businessmen hostile to the king. The Hawaiian League itself had two factions: a conservative wing that sought to bring some checks and balances to the almost absolute power of the king, and a militant branch that wanted nothing less than to overthrow the monarchy and annex the islands to the United States.

On June 30, the Hawaiian League held a huge rally, with inflammatory speakers who purposely worked the crowd into a frenzied mob. Hundreds of men took to the streets. They stormed Premier Gibson's house and that of his son-in-law, and dragged both men out with nooses around their necks. Only military intervention by the British Consul saved the men from being lynched. As it was, Gibson suffered a stroke that left him in serious condition; he was taken to a boat bound for San Francisco.

Representatives of the Hawaiian League then confronted Kalākaua. They demanded that he dismiss the Gibson cabinet and sign a new constitution into law — one under which he would reign but not rule. The new constitution made both houses of legislature into elected bodies (under Kalākaua's system, he appointed the members of the House of Nobles) and gave the legislature power to override the king's veto.

Perhaps most troubling, it required that voters own property. This effectively took the vote away from most native Hawaiians and gave it to virtually every Western businessman, even those who weren't citizens. Why did so few Hawaiians own land? For centuries, Hawaiian land had been overseen by the aliʻi and his people — the concept of *owning* land was completely foreign to Hawaiians. When Western businessmen had begun to want to own Hawaiian property (and reap Hawaiian sugar profits), land formerly governed by aliʻi had been parceled out to the Hawaiian people. Native Hawaiians, often unable to read English, had had no understanding of how a piece of paper could mean that they "owned" mountains or lakes or coastland, and they had been happy to sell the deeds to Westerners for cash in hand. In this way, many Hawaiians had ended up homeless in their own country. Now, according to the new constitution, the Westerners had bought up votes along with the land. The running of the country would now be in their hands.

King Kalākaua refused to sign this constitution. Recognizing the power of the Hawaiian League, he assembled representatives of foreign nations, asking them to intervene. None would. On July 6, Kalākaua was forced to sign the new constitution virtually at gunpoint. Consequently, it became known as the Bayonet Constitution.

* * *

DURING THIS TIME, Archie was asked to become Collector of the Customs House — an important job in a nation that depended so heavily on importing and exporting. In the wake of the scandal, Archie was seen as a man of integrity, friendly to the king yet acceptable to the Western community.

It was clear that Archie understood the serious implications of the new constitution: Kaʻiulani couldn't help but notice that he was stomping around and muttering about this state of affairs. Yet, when Kaʻiulani was taken to visit the king, she found *him* surprisingly calm. This is clear in a letter she wrote to her aunt, in which she said casually, "I went to see Papa Mō̄ī and he told me you would soon be home so I will not write much. . . . My new governess is with me now, and I have to study many things so I am busy all day. . . ." The only hint that anything was wrong was when she mentioned that "Kapena [the Hawaiian who had run the Customs House] is put out."

Did Kaʻiulani not understand the impact of what had happened? Or did she decide that it was out of her hands — that her father, and soon Aunt Lydia, would be outraged enough for all of them? Even decades later, it was clear that neither Archie Cleghorn nor Lydia Liliʻuokalani ever forgave Kalākaua for what they considered his self-indulgence and lapses in judgment that resulted in a much weakened monarchy.

The queen and her companions returned at the beginning of August. September brought further sadness to the Kalākaua family: Edward, the middle boy of the Three Princes, was sent home ill from school in San Mateo, California. He died of scarlet fever shortly after arriving in the Islands.

Death was becoming a fact of Kaʻiulani's life. Of the Four Sacred Ones, only two remained; now there were "Three Princes" no more. Kaʻiulani felt the losses deeply.

* * *

1888 WAS A quiet year for the princess, though a difficult one for the king. The Westerners in the legislature, euphoric with their new power, tried to deny the king's ability to veto any legislation. In-censed, Kalākaua went to the Big Island and did not return until the Supreme Court upheld this privilege.

The king was also forced to renegotiate the Reciprocity Treaty, which gave Hawaiian sugar favored entry into the American market. Before the United States would agree to extend the privilege, he had to allow the U.S. sole access to the harbor at the mouth of the Pearl River. No one had any idea of the role that American ships in Pearl Harbor would eventually play in history.

*　　*　　*

EARLY ONE EVENING in March, the princess carefully dressed for an official outing. On this occasion, she would be joined by Aunt Lydia and Mr. Lorrin Thurston, who was Minister of the Interior. Together they would make the two-hour trip to a power station in the valley outside of the city.

Even though Ka'iulani was excited, she was a bit apprehensive about traveling in the company of Mr. Thurston. The grandson of Congregational missionaries, he was one of the Hawaiian League's most vocal advocates of overthrowing the monarchy. He was also no friend of Archie Cleghorn's. After Likelike's death, Thurston, a lawyer, had personally seen to it that Archie had to go to court to become legal guardian of Ka'iulani — his own daughter!

But this occasion was momentous enough that the anti-Royalist and the two princesses put their differences aside. They were all excited by the time they arrived at the power station. Precisely at seven o'clock, the superintendent of the station and his assistant helped Princess Ka'iulani onto a chair. Then she threw a switch that sent power flowing — and suddenly, all of Honolulu was shining with electric lights. The island kingdom was ahead of many other countries in acquiring this new invention.

Lorrin Thurston, Minister of the Interior and grandson of Asa Thurston, one of the first Protestant missionaries in Hawaiʻi

*　　*　　*

AS DIFFICULT AS sea travel was, many well-known figures came to visit Hawaiʻi, including King Oskar of Sweden and the American humorist Mark Twain. As the months passed and 1889 approached, a buzz ran through Oʻahu society: the famed Scottish writer Robert Louis Stevenson was on his way to the Islands.

Stevenson had already published several well-known books, including *Treasure Island* and *The Strange Case of Dr. Jekyll and Mr. Hyde.* He suffered from tuberculosis, and doctors had advised him to leave the cold, damp climate of his native Scotland for the balmier weather of the South Seas. Along with his mother, his wife, and her family, he had traveled to Samoa and Tahiti. Now he was going to visit Hawaiʻi.

The night that Stevenson's yacht *Casco* finally arrived (but before anyone had disembarked), Kaʻiulani attended a gala party on a neighboring boat. With Chinese lanterns bobbing, many of the guests sang to the accompaniment of the piano or other instruments. Kaʻiulani's best friend and half-sister, Annie Cleghorn, sang "The Gypsy Countess," and Kaʻiulani joined in a ukulele trio. They all strained unsuccessfully to see any sign of the international celebrity.

When the frail but spirited Stevenson finally came ashore and settled in Waikīkī, he and his family became the center of the busy social scene. In fact, it was all his wife could do to keep people away long enough for her husband to be able to work on his current novel, *The Master of Ballantrae*.

He quickly became friends with King Kalākaua and Princess Liliʻuokalani. They invited each other to lavish dinners and presented each other with expensive gifts. At thirteen, Kaʻiulani was considered too young to be invited to such social events. Yet it was hard to be content just hearing stories about what an interesting man the famous writer was.

But if Stevenson had his choice, he would rather sit and have an intimate talk with a friend than be the center of a party.

And so it was on one February day that a tall, almost comically thin man in white flannels (a fashionable suit material) walked down the long shaded drive to ʻĀinahau. There he found the young princess with long black hair and flashing eyes reading under her banyan tree.

"Good afternoon," he said. "Mr. Cleghorn did me the honor of suggesting I might call. My name is — "

"I know," said Kaʻiulani with a shy smile. "You're Mr. Stevenson."

King Kalākaua (background, center) seated beside his sister, Princess Liliʻuokalani,
at a lūʻau given for the Stevenson family in 1889

The poet joined the princess under the banyan tree, and a magical friendship began. They both had vivid imaginations, inquiring minds, and sly senses of humor. Both were actually shy, though forced to spend much time in the public spotlight. Both were interested in books and ideas. Kaʻiulani was fascinated by the worlds Stevenson had seen in his travels; Stevenson was captivated by the history and gentle charm of the Hawaiians.

So while Mr. Stevenson grudgingly fulfilled his social obligations, his favorite hours were those spent in happy conversation with Kaʻiulani. He gave his newfound friend a wonderful gift: a large, beautiful music box with intricate orchestration (which today can be seen in the Hulihee Palace on the Big Island).

The friendship and esteem of this great writer did much for

At thirteen, Princess Ka'iulani was fascinated by Robert Louis Stevenson. He called her "The little royal maid."

Ka'iulani's self-confidence. With him, she felt witty and bright and curious. Even obeying rules of etiquette became an exercise in fun, as seen in the "proper" notes they wrote each other:

Mr. Stevenson: Dear Sir:

Your kind note has come. I thank you for it. Papa and I would like to have you come to our home on Tuesday next for dinner and Papa promises good Scotch "kaukau" for all you folks.

My pony Fairie has a cold today so I cannot go riding. When you come please bring with you your flute. I am your most affectionate and obedient friend.

Ka'iulani C.

69

And in return:

> Dearest Child:
> I do most heartily welcome the opportunity to dine with you and your respected father on the evening of Tuesday the 23 [rd]. . . . I hope you have found time to read through the book which I have given you.
>
> Most respectfully,
> Robert L. Stevenson

It was a friendship which came at a fortuitous time.

For in March, a decision was made that sent the normally adventurous princess into a panic.

King Kalākaua, knowing that the monarchy rested on the ability of future kings and queens to be able to match wits with well-educated foreigners, announced that Kaʻiulani would be sent abroad to continue her education.

For the thirteen-year-old, it was hard to explain her anxiety, even to herself. Yes, the Three Princes had attended a military school in California, and Koa and Kūhiō were attending a university in England. They both enjoyed their travels. But Kaʻiulani had never left her island kingdom. Not only that, but she feared that while Papa Mōʻī claimed that the trip would last only a year, her mother's prophecy would prove true, and the trip would turn into long-term banishment.

She fought against the king's pronouncement.

But there are things in life that even a princess cannot change. A school in England was chosen, and May 10 was set as her sailing date.

And there was more upsetting news: in April, word came from the leper colony on the island of Molokaʻi that Father Damien, the

Annie Cleghorn, Ka'iulani's half-sister and best friend, in a photograph taken in January 1889 — just a few months before she and the princess left for England

Catholic priest who had selflessly ministered to the ill, had himself died of leprosy.

But two things *did* brighten Ka'iulani's spirits. First, her beloved half-sister Annie agreed to go with her to England as her companion. While history does not make much mention of Archie's first "common-law" wife, Elisabeth Lapeka, their three daughters were an important part of Archie's — and Ka'iulani's — life. While Rose and Helen were considerably older and married, Annie was as much like a sister to Ka'iulani as a nonroyal could be. Annie promised to stay in London for as many months as it took to help Ka'iulani settle in and adjust.

And second, there were the wonderful hours Robert Louis Stevenson spent with her, painting vivid word portraits of his native Britain, to which Kaʻiulani would soon sail. He reminded her that she wasn't just leaving her mother's people; she was going to her father's people.

But privately, Stevenson was sorry to lose Kaʻiulani's company. As he wrote to his French friend, W. H. Low, "If you want to cease to be a republican, see my little Kaʻiulani as she passes through. I wear the colours of the little royal maid. Oh, Low, how I love the Polynesians!"

As the day of her departure drew closer, Kaʻiulani's new wardrobe was assembled. She'd never had winter clothes before! But even though Annie chatted excitedly about their adventures to come, and their father was preparing to accompany them as far as San Francisco, nothing could lift Kaʻiulani's depression.

She went weekly to St. Andrew's, praying that her sentence might be lifted. That prayer wasn't answered. Instead, she was given new strength to do what she must.

For two days before the ship sailed, the thirteen-year-old princess summoned all the courage that was required of her. She went with her father to pay farewell calls to all the members of the legislature and other important government officials. She was greeted with grace and good wishes even in the parlors of the staunchest anti-Royalists. These calls reminded them that Kaʻiulani was the heir presumptive, that she would take her education seriously — and that she would one day return to her beloved Islands. The last calls were saved for close family and friends, including Miss Gardinier — now Mrs. Heydtmann — and her new baby.

Often as she prepared for the dreaded trip, Kaʻiulani opened her autograph book and read what Mr. Stevenson had written there:

Forth from her land to mine she goes,
The island maid, the island rose,
Light of heart and bright of face,
The daughter of a double race.

Her islands here in southern sun
Shall mourn their Kaʻiulani gone,
And I, in her dear banyan's shade,
Look vainly for my little maid.

But our Scots islands far away
Shall glitter with unwonted day,
And cast for once their tempest by
To smile in Kaʻiulani's eye.

Written in April to Kaʻiulani in the April of her age, and at
Waikīkī within easy walk of Kaʻiulani's banyan. When she comes
to my land and her father's and the rain beats upon the window
(as I fear it will) let her look at this page; it will be like a weed
gathered and preserved at home; and she will remember her own
islands, and the shadow of the mighty tree; and she will hear the
peacocks screaming in the dusk and the wind blowing in the
palms.

*   *   *

ON THE DAY of the princess's sailing, the docks were lined with
thousands of well-wishers. Kaʻiulani did her very best to smile as she
boarded the *S. S. Umatilla* with Annie and their father and Mrs.
T. R. Walker, who was sailing with her two small children and would
act as Kaʻiulani's chaperone to England.

Kaʻiulani's banyan tree
at ʻĀinahau, a symbol
of all that she would miss
in England

Usually, when ships sailed to and from Honolulu, the Royal Hawaiian Band played "Aloha ʻOe." But today, in honor of the royalty
aboard, as the gangplank was pulled up, they launched into the national anthem, "Hawaiʻi Ponoʻī."

Waves, shouts, and tears mingled on the dock as Hawaiians and
foreigners alike bid farewell to their princess.

On board, Kaʻiulani waved farewell to her subjects for as long as propriety demanded.

Then she fled from the deck to her cabin and burst into tears.

The princess in San Francisco in May 1889

FIVE

The New World

Ka'iulani spent the weeklong crossing from Honolulu to San Francisco that mid-May of 1889 overcome with seasickness. For days on end she stayed, wretched, in her cabin.

Many friends of Hawai'i lived in San Francisco; in fact, many had houses in both places. It was easy to see why Likelike had liked this city by the bay so much. Whenever Hawaiian royalty arrived, they were treated like royalty. The welcome for Ka'iulani was no less warm. Dinners, sight-seeing, and entertainments were planned. But Ka'iulani had not yet fought her way out of her depression. She often chose to wear black, and photographic portraits taken of her there show a sad and thoughtful young woman, missing the sparkle that had shone through earlier photos.

The day that Ka'iulani, Annie, and the Walkers boarded the train for New York via Chicago, Archie returned to Honolulu.

The sheer breadth of the United States and the modern buildings in Chicago were eye-opening for the half-sisters. But Ka'iulani's interest was fully piqued when they reached New York City in early June.

It was hard for them to take in the immensity of the city and the thoroughfares crowded with horses and carriages. They were staying in the Brevoort Hotel at the bottom of fashionable Fifth Avenue, and the glittering homes, restaurants, and mansions they passed seemed wonderful, each one more splendid than the last. And nowhere else — not in San Francisco, not in Chicago — had Ka'iulani seen so many people! It seemed to her that she had passed as many en route from the train to the hotel as lived in all of Hawai'i.

But she and her fellow travelers didn't have much time to explore New York; their ship sailed for England within days.

Ka'iulani's steamship docked in Liverpool on June 17, 1889. That same day, she, Annie, and the Walkers boarded the train for Manchester, where they spent the night.

The very next day, June 18, they arrived in London.

Ka'iulani had spent so much time imagining the sights and sounds of London that it had seemed like a fairy-tale land to her. To finally be in the city where Queen Victoria reigned was tremendously exciting. Although she was still homesick, the remnants of her depression lifted, and her adventurous spirit bubbled forth once again.

She and Annie would long remember the full, exciting week they spent there. They visited art galleries, where Ka'iulani was especially impressed by original paintings by Titian, Rubens, and Sir Joshua Reynolds, the renowned English portrait painter. They visited the Tower of London and the Crystal Palace, called one of the Seven Wonders of the World because of its great size and innovative use of glass and iron. They rode the underground railway and went to the theater almost every night. They saw the Shah of Persia traveling through town, and even saw Queen Victoria's own carriage.

It was an exciting time in London — the cusp of the "Belle Epoch," the beautiful years. It was a time when art and culture flourished. New ways of thought led to individual freedoms in art and society. Women were among those finding a new freedom — much of which, surprisingly, was due to the invention of the bicycle, which allowed "polite" women the freedom to travel unchaperoned for the first time. The fashionable dress of the day for women was a wide-shouldered blouse with muttonchop sleeves, cinched with a corset and a wide belt into a tiny waist. Rakish boater hats were very popular.

While she adored London, Ka'iulani was apprehensive about starting school in mid-September at Great Harrowden Hall. This was a school for young ladies in Northamptonshire, nearly seventy miles outside of London. The imposing square building had smaller wings on either side. Four centuries old, it had been built as a barony. Ka'iulani had never attended school with other pupils before. Although Annie stayed on as her companion, there was certainly no Kanoah to rush in and pick up fallen books!

But Ka'iulani would benefit from this experience, strange as it felt at first. She would find lifelong friends in England and at Great Harrowden Hall. Whether or not she had found any by her fourteenth birthday that first October away from home, it's certain that she felt much more a young woman of the world than she had the year before.

*   *   *

CHRISTMAS IN LONDON was a magical season. There Ka'iulani joined dapper, handsome Koa, who was now twenty-one. (Kūhiō

One of the challenges Kaʻiulani faced in England: Great Harrowden Hall

was also attending school in England, but he was unable to join them.) Kaʻiulani realized she felt a bit nervous about seeing her cousin. Why did she have butterflies about seeing good old Koa, whom she'd known since birth?

Perhaps things had changed. For the first time, Kaʻiulani felt she was meeting him on more equal footing. He was a sophisticated young man — but she was now a well-traveled young woman. Their conversation was much more that of equals — very different from what it had been when she was a little girl who'd never left the Islands.

That December, she and Koa had a wonderful time. It's interesting to note that, while they were in England, the two Hawaiian aliʻi called each other by the English parts of their names: Kaʻiulani

80

Prince Koa, no longer the
schoolboy Ka'iulani had
once known

and Kawānanakoa became Vike and David. But even David, seemingly so mature and sophisticated, admitted that he was homesick and wished he could return to Honolulu.

*   *   *

ALTHOUGH SCHOOL WAS hard work, Ka'iulani's first winter wasn't as bad as she expected it to be. In March, she wrote to the queen, "We have had some very cold weather, I rather like it when you can roast yourself by the fire, but it is no joke out in the open air. I think I would like it moderately cold, not quite as cold as it is now. I wonder what we would do if we had it as cold at home as it is here?"

She was also able to report that she was making progress in her French lessons: "Now I am third in my French class," she said proudly.

That spring, Ka'iulani decided to be confirmed in the Anglican faith by the Bishop of Leicester. She took this declaration of her Christian faith seriously.

*   *   *

BACK IN HAWAI'I, things were improving politically for the king. The previous autumn, a revolution to restore him to full power had been put down, but when the new legislature was elected, many of the pro-royalty candidates won.

However, worrisome news arrived via English friends who returned from the Islands: the king was said to be in ill health.

Hoping to cheer him up, Ka'iulani painted him a small picture and sent it back to Honolulu, in care of Mama Mō'ī. "I hope he will soon get well again. Please give him my love," she instructed the queen.

October came, and with it not only Ka'iulani's fifteenth birthday celebration but the event she had dreaded: Annie's departure. She had spent a year with Ka'iulani, helping her to adjust. After she left, the princess was completely on her own.

That fall, she got a letter from King Kalākaua himself. After asking about her schooling, he added a cryptic warning: "Be on guard against certain enemies I do not feel free to name in writing."

Ka'iulani was alarmed. She wrote back immediately: "I am quite at a loss to know to whom you refer as not to be relied upon —

I wish you could speak more plainly, as I cannot be on my guard unless I know to whom you allude."

But no reply was forthcoming.

In November, she heard reports of the festivities marking King Kalākaua's fifty-fourth birthday, which included parties and a regatta. She couldn't help remembering the big regatta of his grand fiftieth celebration: the royal boat slicing through clear water, the bright sun above, the reefs below. What a contrast to the gray, chilly November weather surrounding her now!

The week after his birthday, Kalākaua sailed for the United States for treaty talks. He was fêted both up north in San Francisco and down south in San Diego — even in Mexico. It seemed things were looking up.

So it was a great shock on January 21 when Ka'iulani was called from class at Great Harrowden Hall and told that her guardian, Theo Davies, had come to the school and was waiting to speak with her. (Mr. Davies, the former British consul to Hawai'i and owner of an important Honolulu business, had taken over her guardianship once Mrs. Hall had delivered her safely to England.)

"Why, Mr. Davies!" she said, always pleased to see the man she considered a good friend. But the solemn look on his face stopped her cheerful greeting. "There's something wrong, isn't there?"

"I'm afraid so," he said. "News has come from the U.S. It seems your uncle, King Kalākaua, has died in San Francisco."

Ka'iulani sat down heavily, stunned.

"This news is not only very sad; it changes everything in the Islands," said Mr. Davies gently. "You may be needed there. It's probably for the best you leave school for a few days. We would be pleased to have you as a guest at Sundown."

Theo Davies, the guardian
who became a second
father to Kaʻiulani

The princess accepted, and returned with Theo Davies to his
home in Hesketch Park, Southport.

As Mr. Davies had foreseen, the king's death had many political
consequences. But Kaʻiulani's first thoughts were of her family's sorrow. That very afternoon she wrote to Aunt Lydia:

Dear Auntie:

I have only just heard the sad news from San Francisco. I cannot
tell my feelings just at present, but Auntie, you can think how I
feel. I little thought when I said goodbye to my dear Uncle nearly
two years ago that it would be the last time I should see his dear

84

Kaʻiulani dressed for the
chill of an English winter

face. Please give my love to Mama Mōʻī and tell her I can fully
sympathize with her.

I cannot write any more, but Auntie, you are the only one left
of my dear Mother's family, so I can ask you to do that little thing
for me.

I must close with love and kisses,

> I remain,
> Your loving niece,
> Kaʻiulani.

Mourners for King Kalākaua crowd the royal burial grounds at Nuʻuanu.

With her reference to the two years she had been gone, Kaʻiulani hoped to remind her aunt that she was only supposed to be away for one. She very much hoped that Mr. Davies was right, and that she would be called home. After all, she and Aunt Lydia were now the only Kalākauas who remained.

* * *

BECAUSE ENGLAND HAD transatlantic cables that carried messages to and from the United States, Kaʻiulani knew of her uncle's death the day after it occurred. But the king's Hawaiian subjects would have no idea until they sighted the ship returning with their king — and realized it was adorned with black bunting.

Kaʻiulani was able to arrange for a wreath of orchids to accompany her uncle's casket on its sad trip home. The message she sent with them read simply, *"Aloha me ka paumake,"* which means, "My love is with the one who is done with dying."

An important man had passed from Hawaiʻi's history. The Hawaiians had lost another high aliʻi. Kaʻiulani had lost another member of her family.

There was nothing to do now but wait to find out what would happen next.

Liliʻuokalani on the day she was proclaimed queen

SIX

Hawai'i's New Queen

When King Kalākaua died, Aunt Lydia became Her Majesty Queen Lili'uokalani, the monarch of the Hawaiian Islands. Lili'uokalani's husband, John Dominis, went from being simply the governor of O'ahu to being prince consort as well.

At eleven A.M. on March 9, the queen and the prince consort arrived in the throne room of 'Iolani Palace, accompanied by the members of the queen's cabinet and a military escort. There they were met by all the members of the House of Nobles. The queen was a committed Anglican, and at her request, a brief prayer was offered.

Then she read the following:

"Nobles of my Kingdom: I have called you together to deliberate on a grave matter of State. Article Twenty-Two of the Constitution calls upon me to appoint a successor to the throne. The same Article calls for the approval of your Honorable Body of my appointment.

"I now announce to you Our beloved Niece, Her Royal Highness Victoria Kawēkiu Lunalilo Kalaninuiahilapalapa Ka'iulani, as my successor to the Throne of the Kingdom, and I hope that your deliberations will lead you to approve of my appointment."

The appointment was resoundingly applauded. Just before noon, the Royal Hawaiian Band greeted the news with the national anthem followed by "The Kaʻiulani March," which had been composed for the princess's christening ceremony. Three formal riders were dispatched to go throughout the city to herald Kaʻiulani's official status. Artillery at the waterfront were cued to fire a salute, which was answered by a twenty-one-gun salute from the American warship *Mohican*.

Even the anti-royalty newspaper, *The Advertiser*, had nothing but praise for the young princess:

> The nomination of Her Royal Highness Princess Victoria Kaʻiulani as Heir Apparent to the throne will receive the hearty endorsement of the entire population, native and foreign. . . . She is now in England . . . pursuing her studies, and if she is allowed to continue them . . . it ought to give her the foundation of an enlightened liberal education which will fit her for the high position which she is destined to fill.

So while Her Royal Highness Victoria Kaʻiulani was saluted and celebrated in Hawaiʻi, Kaʻiulani the student did declensions of French verbs in England and tried to hide her frustration. She felt as though she was living a double life.

She wrote to Koa, who also chafed at being so far away:

> Dear Kawānanakoa,
> Thank you very much for the kind letter which I received yesterday. As I have not had any home letters by the last mail, and I have no instructions to return home at present. I may have letters next week — and if I do go home, I will let you know. How do you like

Cirencester [the English town where he and his brother were attending school], and what is Kūhiō doing? . . .

It wasn't unusual that Ka'iulani would expect to be called back to Hawai'i. When Aunt Lydia was heir apparent, she ruled in King Kalākaua's place when he was away on official business. If Ka'iulani, at fifteen, was too young to rule by herself, surely Aunt Lydia would want her to at least become a visible part of public life. Even though it had taken a death to accomplish it, it seemed at last her exile would end. How hard it was to pay attention in class!

When letters and packages did finally arrive from home, the princess opened them with great eagerness. They included glowing reports of Ka'iulani's official appointment as heir apparent. Named after her, if she should die without children, was David Kawānanakoa and his heirs.

But despite the princess's eagerness to assume her new royal duties, the queen did not call her home. She called Koa home instead.

Why did Aunt Lydia ask David, who was not a blood relative, to return to the Islands, instead of her own niece?

In a way it was the most practical decision to make. At twenty-three, Koa was old enough to take part in government affairs. The queen faced a good deal of prejudice because she was a woman. In fact, Robert Wilcox, the hotheaded patriot who had led the failed revolution to restore Kalākaua's power, made bitter statements disavowing loyalty to the queen, because he had no intention of being ruled by women, whom he called "puppets." The queen knew that Koa would be a visible reminder of male proximity to the throne.

In addition, Queen Lili'uokalani was planning some political maneuvers with which she might not have wanted her niece connected. But it also seems there was another, more hidden reason that Ka'iulani would become aware of only years later.

Prince Koa, who received
the royal summons to
return to the Islands

In any case, when the summons came, it was for Koa; Kaʻiulani was to remain in England and continue her studies.

Kaʻiulani was greatly disappointed by the news. The only thing that kept her from becoming truly depressed was that her father was coming for a visit. She hadn't seen him in two years — since their farewell in San Francisco.

Archie Cleghorn could be stubborn and opinionated, but he could also exude considerable charm when he chose to do so. When he arrived at Great Harrowden Hall, he became a great favorite of the girls as well as the teachers.

Kaʻiulani was delighted to see Papa. Her life changed immediately: the two of them left at once for rooms in the Langham Hotel

Archie Cleghorn went to
visit Ka'iulani in 1891,
shortly after Lili'uokalani
became queen.

on Regent Street in London. From there, they began a busy, happy summer, one in which Ka'iulani was treated not like an anonymous schoolgirl but like the princess that she was.

Archie knew about everything that was going on in the Islands, or so it seemed to his daughter. For the first time she got a detailed report of what was happening. Not all the news was good. The new American minister, John Stevens, who was supposed to impartially represent the United States, was a vocal advocate of American expansionism. He wanted the Islands to cease to be an independent nation and instead become part of his country. This had only fueled the hopes of the radical arm of the Hawaiian League, the organization of Westerners responsible for the "Bayonet Constitution."

However, Queen Lili'uokalani was a stalwart woman and a devout

Christian who shared many of the same values as the Westerners. Certainly she would rule without the scandals caused by her late brother. Archie thought it helped that her husband was Western, and could act both as her advisor and as a liaison with the business community.

Archie was sure that Kaʻiulani would be called home within a year. He talked excitedly of plans to build a grand house at ʻĀinahau — one that would be fitting for a future queen.

This was all such happy news that Kaʻiulani felt she was on the verge of a wonderful life. And, for the next three months, she was correct.

*　　*　　*

ARCHIE WAS IN Britain not only to visit his daughter and his country of origin; he was there on business for the queen. He and Kaʻiulani were soon invited to visit Parliament, Windsor Castle, and the Royal Gardens. They did not meet Queen Victoria; Kaʻiulani's presentation to the queen would be arranged just before she sailed for home.

But they were fêted, entertained, and treated like royalty. When Archie went "back home" to visit Scotland, for example, he and Kaʻiulani stayed for ten days with the Honorable R. A. McFee at Dreghorn Castle. There Princess Kaʻiulani planted two trees to commemorate her visit, as King Kalākaua had done when he had stayed at the castle. Next they went to Glasgow and Edinburgh, Scotland, and returned to London through Wales, where they stayed with Lord and Lady Brassey at Normanhurst, their ancestral home.

Along with much of the English society set, the Cleghorns went to watch the naval maneuvers at Portsmouth, where they stayed for ten days. Kaʻiulani had so much fun on this trip that she was eager to bring Papa with her on their final stop: Sundown, Theo Davies'

Ka'iulani (seated front left) with her father (seated center),
visiting with friends in England

house on the Irish Sea. Theo had been a surrogate parent for her, so Ka'iulani was very happy to have her two fathers together.

Of the Davies' children, two were just a little older than Ka'iulani — Clive and Alice. Ka'iulani felt at home with them and able to be fully herself. There were tennis courts at Sundown, and Ka'iulani took up the sport with great enthusiasm, laughing often and feeling energetic and hopeful. She also attracted a vivacious group of friends of both sexes. They enjoyed her for herself, not because she was a princess, and would remain close to her throughout the coming years.

Although Archie unsuccessfully fought a bad cold during his entire visit, Ka'iulani's only physical problem seemed to be her eyesight. She had mentioned this to her aunt, and the queen was concerned. So when they were back in London, Archie took Ka'iulani to the optom-

Portrait of John Owen
Dominis, Queen
Liliʻuokalaniʻs husband

etrist, where she was fitted with glasses. He reported to Liliʻuokalani: "Kaʻiulani . . . can read all right but she cannot see without glasses any object a few feet away. She is nearsighted, and I am afraid will remain so. I will give you full particulars upon my return."

They weren't prepared for the sad news that reached them in London. Uncle John Dominis, Liliʻuokalani's husband, died suddenly from an illness that hadn't seemed serious. While the couple had not had the happiest of marriages, they had finally reached a place where they were working well together, with the queen relying on him heavily for help with the Western community in Hawaiʻi. He died, as Aunt Lydia would later write, "just at the time I was to need most greatly his guiding hand."

This was a great loss to the family and to the monarchy. Lili'uokalani wrote Ka'iulani about her sorrow from her home, Washington Place, on September 18, 1891:

My Dear Ka'iulani,
You have heard e'er this of the death of your dear Uncle John, from Mrs. Robertson [Ka'iulani's half-sister, Rosie].

I could not write at the time to tell you, for I was so shocked. It all seemed so sudden to me. It is true he had been sick ten weeks but I had no idea he would pass away so soon, for he looked so well that morning. It seems we are having a series of sadnesses in our family for it is only seven months since my dear Brother died, when my husband was taken away — not that only but a short time before Uncle John's death the Queen Dowager Kapi'olani had a stroke of paralysis and is likely to have another.

If it is the father's will in Heaven I must submit for the Bible teaches us "he doeth all things well."

You and Papa are all that is left to me.

I shall look forward to the time when you [can] finish your studies with all due satisfaction to your teachers, and then come home and live a life of usefulness to your people.

Ka'iulani had already written to express her grief. The death was a blow to Archie as well. He and John had been compatriots within the Kalākaua family.

When Kalākaua had been king, Archie had assumed the governorship of O'ahu when John was away, so it seemed natural to suppose that he would be asked to do so again for Lili'uokalani. With that in mind, Archie planned to return to the Islands at the beginning of October. While he would not be taking Ka'iulani with him, he promised he would try to facilitate her return as soon as possible.

The Cleghorns' hotel in London was a gathering place for friends from Hawai'i who were in England. These friends helped lift their spirits and also brought news from home. One piece of news they heard from several quarters was about the new governor of O'ahu: the queen planned to appoint David Kawānanakoa.

While Ka'iulani loved Koa, she felt deeply hurt for her father, who had counted on the "promotion." Flexing her own political power for the first time, she wrote to Lili'uokalani, "I hear from many people that David is to have the Governorship. Please do not think me very forward, but I should so like Father to have it. I have not asked you for anything before, but if you can possibly grant this, I should be so grateful."

In the same letter, she offered a not-so-veiled plea for herself: "When I come home, I shall try to help you as much as I can, tho' it will not be much as I don't understand State Affairs."

Shortly before Archie sailed, Archie and Ka'iulani were invited to dine with the Irish playwright John Millington Synge, a gentleman Ka'iulani enjoyed very much. On Archie's last night, they had dinner with friends from Hawai'i, Lord and Lady Wiseman. (Lord Wiseman had been the captain of the *Caroline,* the ship Kalākaua had welcomed with the ball that celebrated the installation of electric lights at the palace.) Also joining them were the Parker girls, the daughters of Samuel Parker, the successful Big Island rancher. When Ka'iulani had visited the Parker ranch as a child, she'd felt that the Parker girls were much older and more sophisticated than she. Now she was finally catching up.

*   *   *

ARCHIE SAILED, AS planned, on October third. It was tremendously hard for Ka'iulani to return to school, and she admitted as much to her aunt: "You can fancy how lonely I shall feel without him. . . . I have been so very happy these last few weeks. I do not know how I shall be able to settle down to lessons again."

Back home, Ka'iulani's petition was granted: Archie became governor of O'ahu. He also began work on the new, grander house at 'Āinahau, fit for the crown princess and, someday, Queen Ka'iulani. (Ka'iulani, who was exchanging letters with Lili'uokalani on a regular basis, reported, "I'm so glad. . . . It has always been my ambition to have a house at Waikīkī worthy of the beautiful gardens!")

And there was other news from home: Her half-sister Annie had gotten married and had a baby. How Ka'iulani longed to see them! But she enjoyed spending Christmas and New Year's with the Davies at Sundown.

Early the next year, Mr. Davies decided Ka'iulani had gotten the best out of Great Harrowden Hall, and he made arrangements for her to be "finished" under the tutelage of a Mrs. Rooke down in Brighton. This was happy news for Ka'iulani, especially because her good friend, Alice Davies, would accompany her for the first few weeks.

Mrs. Rooke lived in a fashionable row house on Cambridge Street in Brighton, a popular vacation spot for high society, down south on the English Channel. The house was next door to a church, and Ka'iulani especially loved hearing the boys' choir rehearsing. The music transported her and buoyed her faith. She loved being on the water again, the "bracing sea air" giving her renewed energy.

At first her lessons were in French, German, English, and grammar, with additional lessons in music (she had a "sweet soprano voice") and painting, for which she also showed a talent.

However, when a friend from home sent Ka'iulani the new book entitled *A Brief History of the Hawaiian People* by W. D. Alexander, she read it eagerly and was much sobered by how little she'd

The church of St. Martyn's

known about her people's past. She soon insisted that world history be added to her curriculum.

Mrs. Rooke also had a small house with lovely gardens on the island of Jersey in the English Channel between England and France. Kaʻiulani was happy to take a holiday there, even though she was haunted by her old tendency to be seasick on the way over. The island reminded her so much of Hawaiʻi that it was a bittersweet experience.

While staying on Jersey, Kaʻiulani attended St. Martyn's, an Episcopal church, twice on Sundays. The early service was in French, the latter in English. She was pleased that she understood both! She was sorry to return to Brighton after only two weeks.

If a young lady (especially a princess) was to be considered "finished," she was also taught dancing and "deportment." So these

The island of Jersey

were added to Ka'iulani's other lessons. She reported, "Last Saturday I had my first lesson in dancing and general deportment, which I found highly amusing. My friends tell me that I carry myself so much better when I am walking in the street than in a drawing room, so at the present moment I am doing my very best to walk into a room quietly and gracefully."

When Ka'iulani spent time at Sundown with the Davies family, she often heard Mr. Davies complaining about the U.S. minister to Hawai'i, John Stevens, whom he called "a snake in the grass." Stevens remained dedicated to taking over the Islands. However, the Royalists had won a small majority in the elections. Aunt Lydia was a Christian and acted like one, so the Westerners had no complaint

101

there. Their greatest concern about the queen was that she was keeping company with so many native Hawaiians, who, of course, wanted to have a voice in the future of their nation.

Aunt Lydia wrote to her niece that she was considering establishing a new constitution by fiat, just as her predecessor, Kamehameha IV, had done thirty years earlier. The most grievous complaint of the native Hawaiians was about the voter qualifications, which allowed only landowners to vote. Many native Hawaiians had sold their land deeds to foreigners, and foreign landowners were allowed to vote whether they became Hawaiian citizens or not! Naturally, foreign voters elected foreign officials. This meant that the elected government represented only a very small percentage of Hawai'i's people.

*　　*　　*

WHILE ANTAGONISTIC POLITICS as usual went on back in Hawai'i, Ka'iulani was focused on one glorious fact — she was finally going home!

She would stay in England through the Christmas season. Then she would travel the continent of Europe for two months. ("The Tour" was commonly expected of young ladies about to "come out" into society.) After that, she would be presented to Queen Victoria.

Then — then she'd sail for home! She would be in Hawai'i for her eighteenth birthday. There she would take her place at the queen's side and prepare for her role in history.

She was giddy with the news.

The Davies invited her to spend the summer with them. Ka'iulani wrote happily to the queen that "I am having such very pretty summer dresses made. I do like pretty, dainty things. All the ladies are wearing dresses made like men's clothes. I do dislike them so, they look so very manly."

The princess in one of the summer dresses she loved

Ka'iulani spent a wonderful summer with the Davies. A family who took their own Christian faith seriously, they helped open the princess's eyes to the great poverty that had come to England as a result of the Industrial Revolution. (While it made some people very rich, it made others — especially factory workers — very poor.) Once she began paying closer attention, Ka'iulani saw people living in poverty all around her, and it broke her heart.

She and Alice (the Davies' oldest daughter) threw their energy into raising funds for charity, and they were both successful. Queen Lili'uokalani was pleased with her niece's work and sent a generous contribution. In a letter home, Ka'iulani noted that even though she'd raised four hundred pounds (a large sum in those days!), she hoped to raise more. "I wish I could do more for good works."

She was back in Brighton for her seventeenth birthday. To celebrate, Mrs. Rooke gave her a copy of a painting she'd longed for called *Soul's Awakening*. Ka'iulani wrote to the queen, "It is such a beautiful picture. I have always wished to have it, but I have never had enough money. It hangs opposite my bed so that the first thing I see in the morning is the girl's lovely face. I received quite a number of presents and such a lot of letters. I spent a very happy day in spite of being such a long way from home." (On the topic of money, she reluctantly continued, "I hear that you wish Father to be Governor, but to give up the Customs House. Auntie, we cannot do without his salary for that, as the salary of Governor is only half the other. My education and stay in England is costing him something, and Oh Auntie! I do not want him to get into debt. Please do not be offended with me.")

Ka'iulani also received a copy of the October issue of the magazine *Paradise of the Pacific*, which ran an article about her. It told the story of her childhood — Ka'iulani found this quite amusing — and concluded, "None knew her but to love her, None named her but to praise." Although the article was flattering, Ka'iulani thought the best part of it was the ending, which happily looked forward to the imminent "return home of Hawai'i's Hope, to celebrate her eighteenth birthday in the land of her race." Yes! Her imminent return was a published fact.

The rest of autumn flew past. For Christmas, she was invited back to stay with Lord and Lady Wiseman at their home, Priory Rittle. She thought them "gentle people" with refined manners, and did her best to rise to the occasion.

It was a joyous holiday. A date was set for Princess Ka'iulani to be received by Queen Victoria — the one person in the world the princess most wanted to meet. And the Hawaiian legislature had approved four thousand pounds for her return trip.

It was all becoming reality! Plans were breathlessly made for her trip through Europe. The Wisemans took a proprietary interest in the beautiful young woman — as did the Davies — and Lady Wiseman threw herself into helping Ka'iulani plan and order her new wardrobe.

Her days as a schoolgirl were finally over; her life as a working princess had begun.

After Christmas, she returned to the Davies' home to make final preparations for her trip.

It was there, on Monday, January 30, that Theo Davies called her into the library. She joined him happily by the fire, but was quickly confused by the heaviness with which he spoke and the unfathomable sorrow in the confident man's stance. She thought briefly that it reminded her of when he'd come to Great Harrowden Hall to tell her of King Kalākaua's death.

"Ka'iulani, I have received some telegrams," he began.

And then his voice broke. He did not know how to go on, so he silently handed her the three opened documents.

The three telegrams put together contained only eight words. They were words which gave Ka'iulani such a physical shock that she would never fully recover from it. Some have conjectured that actual physical harm was done to her heart. In any case, it's true that from that day on the spirited, energetic young woman would be plagued with poor health and frequent migraines.

The first telegram read: *Queen Deposed.*

The second: *Monarchy Abrogated.*

The third: *Break news to Princess.*

Ka'iulani was Crown Princess of Hawai'i no longer.

A formal portrait of the queen, with the royal cape draped behind her

SEVEN

On the World Stage

Ka'iulani soon pieced together the story of the overthrow from letters and newspaper articles that arrived.

By the end of the last legislative session, Aunt Lydia had skillfully maneuvered to have her Reformer-based cabinet voted out for want of confidence. She had replaced these men with four of her own choosing, men she counted on to be loyal to her goals.

Many citizens had been petitioning her to end the injustices of the "Bayonet Constitution" and replace it with one friendlier to the native Hawaiians, one in which every (male) citizen could vote.* Such a constitution would also take much power away from the legislature and give it back to the monarch — for example, if the queen

---

*In many democratic countries such as Great Britain and the U.S., women were beginning to fight for the right to vote, but men (and some women) felt they were not capable of taking on such responsibility. Both Queen Victoria and Queen Lili'uokalani had been in the strange position of ruling a nation but not being allowed to vote.

would veto a law, the legislature could not override her wishes. Lili'uokalani drafted such a document and sent it to the *Hui Kalai'aina,* a Hawaiian patriotic association, giving them the date she would proclaim it by fiat, as Kamehameha IV had proclaimed his constitution.

On Saturday, January 14, the four members of the cabinet hurried to an unexpected meeting with the queen in the Blue Room of the palace. They were rather surprised to find the palace grounds teeming with the members of the *Hui Kalai'aina* in festive attire, obviously expecting a party. But when the queen showed her cabinet the new constitution, they were afraid to sign it. Instead, they tried to persuade the queen to wait a few years until her reign was well-established and the Royalists had better control of the country. Lili'uokalani had no interest in waiting, but she finally realized the cabinet members were not going to sign that day. The meeting ended on an angry note.

Outside, she announced to the eager Hawaiians that the constitution would be law within a few days; they should go ahead with the festive lū'au they had planned.

Two members of the cabinet, Arthur Peterson and John Colburn, panicked, thinking they'd be blamed for the queen's actions. Seeking advice, they chose to look for it in an unlikely place — the law offices of W. O. Smith, a leader of the Americans who wanted to take over the Islands.

The queen's proposed constitution was the match that made the tinder of revolt burst into flame. Excited and passionate, the Reformers formed a "Committee of Safety," allegedly to protect American property in the upcoming struggle.

Three factions of Westerners opposing the queen quickly emerged.

The two cabinet ministers (and many others) only wanted to

Members of the queen's last cabinet: Samuel Parker (upper left), John Colburn (upper right), William Cornwell (lower left), and Arthur Peterson (lower right)

find means to make the queen withdraw the new constitution she was proposing.

A majority of the haole wanted to continue to have a constitutional monarchy — the kind of government Great Britain had — where the monarchy had "checks and balances" with the legislature. Since Liliʻuokalani wanted full power, they favored replacing her with Princess Kaʻiulani and naming a regent to govern until Kaʻiulani came of age.

But the most passionate faction, the Annexationists, led by lawyer (and missionary grandson) Lorrin Thurston, would accept nothing less than the complete overthrow of the Hawaiian government and the annexation of the Islands by the United States.

Charles Wilson, the queen's military marshal, tried to warn her that the Reformers were holding mass meetings and planning a military coup. He wanted permission to use force to disband them. But the queen was not willing to use force, which she feared could lead to loss of life, even though many Hawaiians were alarmed by the situation and were ready to fight.

The newly formed Committee of Safety, however, had no such qualms. They were charged up and ready to go. Men were rallied and guns supplied. U.S. Minister John Stevens, who was supposed to remain neutral, made it clear that he would consider any action by the queen's marshal an act of lawlessness, while considering any Americans who took over the government in need of "protection."

On Sunday, January 15, while loyal Hawaiians filled the palace square, the Reformers had an incendiary meeting only a block away. Liliʻuokalani had been warned to send for her cabinet and military advisors; instead she summoned Hawaiian Christian pastors, and they spent the morning in prayer.

So the savage queen prayed while the sons of Christian missionaries loaded their rifles.

U.S. Minister John Stevens

That afternoon, Queen Liliʻuokalani signed a paper denouncing the new constitution.

Much negotiating was going on behind the scenes. The man the Annexationists wanted to name as the new president, Sanford Dole, was arguing that, yes, the queen should be dethroned, but instead of being named president of a new government, he should be named regent for Princess Kaʻiulani.

Some of the queen's advisors were warning her that the only way to save the throne in the face of the brewing trouble would be to abdicate in favor of Kaʻiulani. But Liliʻuokalani believed in the "divine right" of kings (and queens) — that God had appointed her and meant her to rule. She also didn't really believe that the situation was that critical.

Archie Cleghorn was called in several times to advise the queen. He became frustrated, believing she was being indecisive and unrealistic.

By Monday, believing a coup was inevitable, Archie went to see Annexationist leader Lorrin Thurston. "I do not blame you for what you are proposing to do to Liliʻuokalani," Archie said, "but I wish to have you take into consideration the claim of my daughter, Princess Kaʻiulani."

Lorrin Thurston, who on the day of his greatest "glory" was fighting a bad case of the flu, answered, "You know my regard for Princess Kaʻiulani, Mr. Cleghorn. I think very highly of her. But matters have proceeded too far for your plan to be an adequate answer to this situation. We are going to abrogate the monarchy entirely."

That day, Minister Stevens landed the U.S. Marines who had been shipboard in the harbor and stationed them throughout Honolulu. As they marched up Fort Street, Liliʻuokalani thought of the loyal Hawaiian men and boys who would be wounded and killed — if not by the Marines, then by the rifle companies rallied by the Committee of Safety — if she resisted.

She also remembered that when Admiral George Paulet had seized Hawaiʻi for Britain in 1843, King Kamehameha III had resigned "under protest," and the Islands had been returned. She decided to do the same thing.

And so the Annexationists won without a physical fight. Their representatives took the queen's signed resignation, along with a hurriedly drawn up request for annexation, and sailed for Washington on the first boat out. The queen was not allowed to send anyone to represent her until the next ship left, giving the Annexationists a good head start.

Sanford Dole, who became acting president of Hawai'i

Meanwhile, John Stevens and the American Marines had overseen a peaceful takeover by the "Provisional Government," soon to be known as the "P.G.s." Even within this group, there were mixed feelings about what had happened.

Sanford Dole, the well-respected American, had indeed become the acting president of Hawai'i. To his brother George in California, Dole wrote,

How I have regretted this whole affair, had I my way about the matter I would have used far more tactful ways than the treatment we have thus rendered. I have reiterated time and again my desire

113

that we hold the power of the throne in a trust . . . in the name of the young princess Ka'iulani . . . until she reaches her majority.

He was hoping this could still come about.

The Annexationists may have won the first round. But neither the queen nor her loyal niece was willing to give up without a fight.

*　　*　　*

KA'IULANI WAS DEVASTATED by the news. She got a letter from her father, in which he blamed Lili'uokalani for "all our troubles." He had been called in to advise her, but she hadn't listened; as he explained,

> If the Queen had abdicated the night of the 16th or early on the 17th, the Throne I think could have been saved. But she did not think they would do as they did. . . . I visited her several times that day, [the] 17th, and told her there would be a Provisional Government. Still she held on — and one hour after, the Committee called and told her they had the Government in their hands.

While others saw making Ka'iulani queen as a solution to the violent hatred some haole had for Lili'uokalani, the princess herself wanted only to see her aunt reinstated.

Her guardian, Theo Davies, who had once been British consul to Hawai'i, knew the fight was not yet lost, but that the battle had moved from Honolulu to Washington, D.C. He felt that if they had any hope of saving the country, they had to move quickly.

"Look!" roared Davies about the newspapers now coming from America. "They're saying Hawaiians are uneducated savages, incapable of governing themselves!" His gaze fell on his young ward. "I know of the answer that will end that argument forever. You."

Ka'iulani had felt gravely wounded by the coup in Hawai'i. Even if what Mr. Davies said was true, how would she ever find the courage to stand up against all these determined men? She was only a teenager!

But then she thought of her sisters — Annie, Helen, and Rosie — and their children. She thought of Koa and Kūhiō and all her Hawaiian friends. She remembered the proud heritage of her people. She knew that it was the responsibility of the ali'i to protect and stand up for his or her people. While she might lack the courage to demand rights for herself, when she thought of the Hawaiian people — her people — she felt strong.

So when Theo Davies said he felt they had to travel to the United States to help fight the overthrow, Ka'iulani replied, "Perhaps some day the Hawaiians will say, 'Ka'iulani could have saved us, but she didn't even try!' I will go with you."

The new wardrobe that had been so carefully readied for touring Europe suddenly had a new purpose — to dress an educated, distinguished princess who was, in a sense, going to war. The seventeen-year-old, who so recently had had the luxury of giggling about trying to properly enter a drawing room, was suddenly being asked to walk onto the stage of history.

Together, Ka'iulani and Mr. Davies came up with a plan. The first salvo, the warning shot aimed toward the P.G.s, was a statement of her intent, published in the London papers:

> Four years ago, at the request of Mr. Thurston, then a Hawaiian Cabinet Minister, I was sent away to England to be educated privately and fitted to the position which by the Constitution of Hawai'i I was to inherit. For all these years I have patiently and in exile striven to fit myself for my return this year to my native

Lorrin Thurston, whom Ka'iulani implicated in her statement to the London press

country. I am now told that Mr. Thurston is in Washington asking you to take away my flag and my throne. No one tells me even this officially. Have I done anything wrong, that this wrong should be done to me and my people? I am coming to Washington to plead for my throne, my nation and my flag. Will not the great American people hear me?

Davies had cabled the queen's representatives in the United States — her minister to Washington, Dr. John Mott-Smith, her former minister of finance, E. C. MacFarlane, and her lawyer, Paul Neumann — that he and the princess were coming to join the fight. Dr. Mott-Smith cabled back, "Cannot use help yet."

116

But if they waited any longer, the fight might be lost.

In late February, Kaʻiulani set sail with Mr. and Mrs. Davies, their daughter Alice, and a companion/maid named Miss Whartoff (and with Kaʻiulani's thirteen trunks and nine bags) on the oceanliner *Teutonic,* bound for New York.

On the passage across, the young princess wrote and rehearsed her speech with Mr. Davies. She drew strength from the fact that Koa was already in the United States fighting the annexation. She hoped she would make her handsome friend and fellow aliʻi proud of her.

She, Alice, and Mrs. Davies carefully chose the dress she would wear when the ship docked. She needed to look like a stylish young woman, yet someone to be taken seriously.

She didn't feel ready to answer reporters' questions, fearing that one misstatement could have grave consequences. So they agreed that she would read the speech, and Mr. Davies, a seasoned diplomat, would field questions.

Kaʻiulani felt more and more nervous as they approached New York. As the ship entered the harbor, Dr. Mott-Smith and Mr. MacFarlane took a boat out to meet them. This buoyed her courage.

As the ship landed, Kaʻiulani saw that hordes of reporters were waiting on the pier, eager to catch a glimpse of her and hear what she had to say.

She gave Alice a final hug and walked with Theo Davies to embrace her destiny. She spoke with grace and eloquence:

Seventy years ago, Christian America sent over Christian men and women to give religion and civilization to Hawaiʻi. Today three of the sons of those missionaries are at your capitol, asking you to undo their fathers' work. . . .

Today I, a poor, weak girl, with not one of my people near me

117

and all of these statesmen against me, have the strength to stand up for the rights of my people. Even now I can hear their wail in my heart, and it gives me strength and I am strong . . . strong in the faith of God, strong in the knowledge that I am right. . . .

Ka'iulani's speech clearly came from the heart, and it was well-received. Many questions followed, and Mr. Davies handled them dexterously.

As the carriage with Ka'iulani and the Davies pulled away from the wharf, Theo Davies looked at his young ward with pride. They had achieved their first objective. The American public would not get all their information from the P.G.s! A barbarian princess indeed! Let them try to explain the beautiful, intelligent woman before them!

*   *   *

KA'IULANI WAS RELIEVED that her speech was over and pleased that it had gone well. Already this visit to New York had a very different feel to it than her first one. As she and her traveling companions walked through the lobby and public rooms at the Brevoort Hotel, there were many reporters waiting to discuss "the Hawaiian question" for their newspapers. Now, it seemed, not only was she interested in New York — New York was interested in her.

"The Princess will not be receiving this evening, gentlemen," Mr. Davies was saying, to Ka'iulani's relief. "However, Dr. Mott-Smith, Mr. MacFarlane, and I will be pleased to answer questions."

Ka'iulani knew they had arrived at a fortuitous — and delicate — time. It was President Benjamin Harrison's last few days in office before the inauguration of Grover Cleveland. Harrison had been in favor of annexing Hawai'i and had quickly sent the treaty to Congress.

But it hadn't passed yet.

The princess, determined to defend her homeland

They had to try to persuade the new president to act differently. But neither Koa nor Paul Neumann, the queen's lawyer, had been able to make an appointment with the new president. Certainly there would be many matters — and people — vying for his attention as soon as he took office.

But Ka'iulani was very determined to do what she could for her people.

While she had found the courage to face and try to persuade reporters, politicians, and millions of Americans of her position, she was about to learn one of the hardest lessons in her life. The first opposition she faced would come from her own inner circle — in fact, from within her own family. And it would come the very night of her first triumph.

David Kawānanakoa had come up from Washington, D.C., to pay a courtesy call on Kaʻiulani. She had always counted him among her best friends and closest allies, and in fact, when they'd spent Christmas together in London, it had seemed as though they both had romantic crushes on each other. But when Mr. Davies showed her the newspapers from Washington, she was shocked to find that Koa had spoken against her trip and had questioned her motives for making it.

Queen Liliʻuokalani, who had sent Koa, knew very well that there was a strong movement afoot to replace her with Kaʻiulani. Kaʻiulani herself had never even considered such a thing — she had come to the United States in full support of her aunt. She couldn't believe that Koa could honestly think otherwise.

She was about to learn that being born into a powerful, public family meant that private sentiments and public actions are often at odds. From this day on, it would be obvious that the queen loved her as a niece but was jealous of her as a political rival.

It also seems that Kaʻiulani didn't realize that Koa might still be smarting over the fact that she had persuaded the queen to take the governorship of Oʻahu away from him and give it to her father.

Mr. Davies saw how Koa's remarks to the press had hurt Kaʻiulani. That evening, the prince came to call at their hotel at 8:30. At 10:00, Mr. Davies finally said that Kaʻiulani would see him. If the wait wasn't insulting enough, Koa wasn't invited up to their rooms. Kaʻiulani would see him in the lobby, Mr. Davies informed him.

Kaʻiulani's meeting with Koa, whom she had hoped to impress and to join forces with, was strained and brief. An experience that had seemed like such a political triumph had become a personal disappointment. Kaʻiulani felt strangely hollow.

President Grover Cleveland, the princess's great hope for Hawai'i

EIGHT

The Princess and the President

If Ka'iulani's first night in America had been disappointing in some ways, by the next morning she felt rededicated to her mission.

She was determined to present her people's case to Grover Cleveland himself. But there was no point in going to Washington until after Cleveland was inaugurated as president. Both Mr. Davies and Ka'iulani knew that she must walk a fine line. She must make her presence strongly felt so that the American people, as well as Congress and the president, could be swayed on the Hawaiian question. Yet if she seemed too overtly political, the queen's supporters might think she was engaging in self-promotion. Ka'iulani firmly believed that she should fully support Lili'uokalani. The native Hawaiians should have nothing to divide them; they had to fight as one people for their country.

The day after her arrival, Ka'iulani made a brief tour of New York. All of the newspapers had run very positive accounts of the princess's arrival, and many had run the full text of her statement.

Prince Koa's negative remarks to the press hurt Kaʻiulani deeply — but didn't deter her from her mission.

However, the next morning, the Washington papers printed the remarks Koa had made after visiting his "cousin" in New York. He claimed she was "working in the wrong direction" and was "under the thumb of Theo Davies. . . . Mr. Davies is working against the interests of the Queen, which is in bad taste, to say the least."

Kaʻiulani was furious on a political level — Koa was causing a split among the Royalists, which was the opposite of what needed to happen. But his words stung most on a personal level. He had insinuated that she was still a child, not thinking for herself, when the truth was that she was working so hard for Hawaiʻi! And that it came from Koa. . . . Her heart felt newly broken.

Yet the future of her nation depended upon her showing herself to be a strong yet benevolent leader! So she would be.

*   *   *

GROVER CLEVELAND WOULD be inaugurated as president on Saturday, March 4. The day before, Kaʻiulani and the Davies headed for Boston to visit the Davies' son, Clive, at his college. A reporter joined them on the train. In the article she wrote subsequently, she discussed her interview with Mr. Davies about Hawaiʻi, but she also gave a detailed description of Kaʻiulani, her manner, and what she wore (a tailor-made dress of blue serge and a fashionable hat). Clearly, Americans were becoming very interested in Kaʻiulani — and this was exactly what she hoped for. If Americans could get to know her, Mr. Davies felt they could be persuaded to prevent the injustice threatening the princess and her people.

Clive Davies met them at the station, and they went to the Hotel Brunswick, where Princess Kaʻiulani was given the beautiful Venetian suite.

The next day, while Cleveland was inaugurated, the princess enjoyed her first sleigh-ride, in a Russian sleigh, through the snowy streets of Cambridge and Boston.

It was announced in the Boston papers that she would attend four o'clock vespers at Trinity Church that Sunday. In the morning, she was able to go anonymously with the Davies to St. Paul's Church for a time of quiet worship. Not surprisingly, when they arrived at Trinity Church that afternoon, it was crowded with well-wishers and reporters. What a strange thing it is, Kaʻiulani thought, when the practice of your faith becomes a public occurrence.

Shortly after this, the popular women's magazine *Housekeeper's Weekly* ran a story that discussed Kaʻiulani's faith — among other things. It said,

> The Princess Kaʻiulani is a dignified young woman: tall, slight, straight. She has the soft brown eyes and dark complexion that mark the Hawaiian beauty. Her sight has been affected by over-study and she wears glasses. She has the sweet, musical voice of her race, and is pronounced very attractive by those who have met her. As to her character, a letter from Mr. Davies, her guardian, to her father, gives some interesting points.
>
> "Kaʻiulani," writes Mr. Davies, "is not an idle nor a butterfly girl, and she will want to take life earnestly. Provision should be made for her continuing such studies as she may desire. . . . Another thing — and most important — is that Kaʻiulani is not a mere worldling; she feels that her life is to be one of service to the King of Kings, and that she is to help her own people to live near Him. It is a solemn question for you to ask yourself how you can best help Kaʻiulani in this work. . . . I know it is Kaʻiulani's great desire to help the Hawaiian girls into lives of Christianity and purity."

On Monday and Tuesday, Kaʻiulani was a purposefully public princess. She sat for a portrait with a well-known photographer and visited the Massachusetts Institute of Technology — Clive's school — and Wellesley College, where it was rumored she had considered attending. (This helped soften the fact that she had an English education; some Americans feared British influence in Hawaiʻi.)

Most important was the large reception held for her, attended by Hawaiian friends in Boston, politicians, and dignitaries — and, of course, the press. Again, reporters described Kaʻiulani's clothes (a gown of ivory silk, strewn with blossoms and trailing vines in turquoise; the skirt trimmed with rows of turquoise satin-ribbon ruching), her hairstyle (a Greek knot), and her demeanor.

One newspaper told how "the Princess begins each sentence with a demure, wholly English air, as if not feeling quite sure that it is decorous for her to express her opinion, and then loses her shyness and speaks enthusiastically until the next question, when her eyes drop and she is the shy school girl again — a manner as fetching as it is un-American." This captivating technique would be put to good use by another young princess, Diana, nearly a century later.

Clive had come with some of his friends from school. These college men were entranced by Kaʻiulani, and they surrounded her chair "like an honor guard" for the duration of the reception. A reporter from another paper overheard one of these students tell the princess he had been born in Hawaiʻi. Kaʻiulani turned to him, the paper said, "with a pretty little showing of sovereignty, and claimed, 'Why then, you belong to me!'"

But the next day, while all the papers ran glowing stories about the princess, an article on the front page of the *Boston Globe* attacked the pension discussed for the dethroned Liliʻuokalani. The writer fumed, "Somehow or other, [offering compensation] doesn't compare over and above favorably with the straightforward ways of other days when the strong annexed the weak by right of might and disdained to bribe anyone into pocketing the injury in silence."

It seemed there were still those Americans who believed that "might equals right." This only strengthened Kaʻiulani's resolve.

* * *

ON WEDNESDAY, THE princess finally boarded a train for Washington, D.C. There she checked into the Arlington Hotel, where she

Ka'iulani with Theo Davies in Boston

was given the suite of rooms recently occupied by the famous actress Sarah Bernhardt.

Most seventeen-year-olds who have felt betrayed by a young man at least get to brood in the privacy of their room. But this was a privilege Ka'iulani didn't have.

Her new celebrity had preceded her, and reporters were waiting for her at the hotel. Waiting for her, too, was Prince David (as the American papers called Kawānanakoa), with a lei of roses as a peace offering. The Davies chatted with him amicably. Ka'iulani accepted the lei and the traditional kiss that accompanied it, but she could not forget what Koa had said to the newspapers after their last meeting. She made a few painfully polite remarks to him — then pointedly asked to be taken to her rooms. Her feelings about Koa were so strong that she couldn't even bear to talk to him.

As Ka'iulani was shown through the lobby to her suite, eager reporters showered her with questions. Frances Folsom Cleveland, the president's young wife, was the other "Woman of the Hour." Was Princess Ka'iulani planning to call on her?

Ka'iulani smiled but pointed out that she was in the United States as a private citizen. As such, she had not received an invitation to the White House.

Knowing the story that would be generated if the two important young women met, one reporter suggested, "But you can call on her any time, in an informal way, and she is almost sure to be pleased to see you."

"I could not do that," Ka'iulani answered, politely but firmly. "No one would call on a private lady with whom they were not acquainted, as you say, informally. And I do not think that the public station of President Cleveland makes any difference."

Theo Davies also gave interviews that afternoon. He made a pointed observation that made the next day's papers: "Over at Wormley's Hotel, where the provisional government commissioners are stopping, I noticed this morning, gentlemen, that the Hawaiian flag is flown. Yet I am told that the *American* flag flies over the Honolulu government buildings. A curious state of affairs!"

The princess herself was of such great interest that even the fact that she came down to dinner at the hotel restaurant was newsworthy. The papers reported what she wore, how she styled her hair (with "fluffy bangs"), how "all heads turned," and how graceful and "democratic" she was.

Everyone in Washington seemed to have taken notice of her visit. The question was, would President Cleveland?

* * *

THE NEXT DAY, a mere five days after he took office, Grover Cleveland made a momentous decision. The papers brought the happy news. "This morning [the president] sent to the Senate a message withdrawing the Hawaiian treaty which was pending."

It was only a first step — but a large step in the right direction! Ka'iulani was ecstatic. She and the Davies could picture the panic among the P.G.s across town. They had arrived so certain that the Annexation Treaty could be rushed through!

The teenager's happiness was so contagious that it wasn't even dampened when Alice, her mouth agape, quoted another of that day's Washington papers. "Ka'iulani — did you know you and Koa are having a serious romance? This paper says you're 'royal lovers. That is, they were expected to be. And if the course of royal love had gone smoothly with other royal affairs in Hawai'i, the Prince was perfectly willing to . . . become the husband of the princess.'"

Ka'iulani couldn't resist laughing as she pictured Koa's face when he read that story!

Mr. Davies found another similar story, in which Dr. Mott-Smith claimed that until recent events, Queen Lili'uokalani had planned on celebrating Ka'iulani and Koa's wedding as soon as Ka'iulani turned twenty-one. Mott-Smith was quoted as saying, however, that if Ka'iulani "has her own way she will marry some young Englishman. It is said that the Princess regards herself as being better than the Prince and she will never consent to a union with a native Hawaiian."

This sobered Ka'iulani immediately. For while she didn't mind (at the moment) the slight aimed at Koa, it hurt her tremendously that anyone would suggest that she thought she was better than native Hawaiians — her own people!

Young as she was, Ka'iulani was getting an instant education in both the pleasures and the trials of public life.

But she and the Davies clung to the good news — the withdrawal of the treaty — and waited to see what would happen next.

* * *

THEY DIDN'T HAVE long to wait. On Monday, the papers carried a bombshell for the P.G.s. Instead of accepting the Annexationists' word for the state of the military coup in Hawai'i, President Cleveland announced that he would send an impartial observer who would report to the president and Congress what had actually transpired. This was the last thing the P.G.s wanted.

As if to underline the president's concern about the morality and legality of the coup, that morning an invitation arrived at the Arlington Hotel. Princess Ka'iulani was invited to visit the White House that very afternoon. She felt vindicated. The queen's advisors — and Koa — hadn't wanted her to come. But she had accomplished what none of them had been able to do.

That afternoon at the Arlington Hotel was a happy flurry of activity for Ka'iulani and the Davies, who, as the princess's escorts, had also been invited. Afternoon gowns were chosen, and

Frances Cleveland, whom
Kaʻiulani pronounced
"sweet and beautiful"

everyone dressed carefully to meet the new president and his wife.

They arrived at the White House promptly at 5:30 and were shown into the Blue Room. (It was only two months earlier, in the Blue Room of ʻIolani Palace, that this whole debacle had begun.)

Both the Clevelands and the princess knew that this was officially a "personal" visit, not a state visit. Consequently, they did not directly discuss politics, although President Cleveland made it clear that he intended to see justice done. Once these sentiments were conveyed and accepted, the personal part of the visit began — and it was delightful. Frances Cleveland and Kaʻiulani were genuinely taken with each other. The president even relaxed enough to show off some of his talents as a mimic.

Kaʻiulani was still aglow with happiness when she arrived back at the Arlington to face a crowd of reporters. In answering their questions, she said, "I was simply infatuated with Mrs. Cleveland. She is very beautiful — but all beautiful women are not sweet, you know. But Mrs. Cleveland is both, and I have fallen in love with her. . . . Mr. Cleveland, too, is very entertaining."

Within the space of a week, she had come into her own. Princess Kaʻiulani of Hawaiʻi had been received at the White House — and was confident enough to speak for herself to reporters.

*   *   *

AS POPULAR AS Kaʻiulani had been before, once she was received at the White House, she became the toast of Washington. She was invited to luncheons and dinners, and partnered by senators and even the French ambassador.

Although she was only going to be in Washington for four more days, the National Geographic Society threw a huge, glittering gala in her honor, attended by the cream of Washington society. She also appeared as the guest of honor at a huge benefit given by the Women's Suffrage Association, which was working to get women the right to vote. So many people clamored to get in to the event that the Washington police received frantic calls for help with crowd control.

Shortly after her meeting with the president, he announced that his Hawaiian representative would be a former congressman named James Blount, who would be given "paramount authority" to investigate the situation. This earned the gentleman the nickname "Paramount Blount." By the time his appointment was announced, he and his wife were already well en route to the Hawaiian Islands.

Kaʻiulani's trip was a resounding success. *Housekeeper's Weekly* (which went to print even before she visited the president) claimed, "The result of her visit to the United States cannot yet be foretold; but it seems not too much to say that there has been some reaction against the disposition to annex the islands, which was so strong at first. Whatever may be the political result, an interest in the country and its people has been awakened, which will not easily die out."

That Saturday, Kaʻiulani and the Davies returned to the Brevoort Hotel in New York. As she prepared to sail back to England, she composed another statement to read to the reporters she knew would gather at the dock. This time she felt much more confident than she had only two weeks ago.

When the time came, she was ready. Smiling warmly at the assembled reporters, she said,

> Before I leave the land, I want to thank all whose kindnesses have made my visit such a happy one. Not only the hundreds of hands I have clasped nor the kind smiles I have seen, but the written words of sympathy that have been sent to me from so many homes, [have] made me feel that whatever happens to me I shall never be a stranger to you again. It was to all the American people I spoke, and they heard me as I knew they would. And now God bless you for it — from the beautiful home where your fair First Lady reigns to the little crippled boy who sent his loving letter and prayer.

Prayers. So many prayers of her own, and others. And it seemed they were being answered as Kaʻiulani had hoped.

Happily she boarded the *Majestic* to return to England — and to await word from home.

Kaʻiulani, still fighting for her beloved Hawaiʻi

NINE

A Nation in the Balance

News from Hawai'i was happy.

On April 1, President Cleveland's representative, James Blount, arrived in O'ahu. He quickly relieved U.S. Minister John Stevens of his duties and sent him packing. He had the U.S. flag lowered from atop the government buildings. Then he set up interviews with those who had participated in the overthrow of the government.

Hawaiians were exultant. When Prince David and the queen's lawyer, Paul Neumann, returned from Washington on April 7, they were fêted at a jubilant celebration at Washington Place, the queen's residence.

But Princess Ka'iulani was the woman of the hour. Her portraits were in the window of a photographer's shop on Fort Street, and they cropped up in other store windows around town. Poems and *meles* (songs) were written about her visit to Washington, such as the following, composed in Hawaiian by Ellen Prendergast:

Let us sing in praise of Kaʻiulani
  Lovely child of Princess Likelike
To our Kaʻiulani . . . rose of ʻĀinahau
  Fair aliʻi, Royal Daughter of Hawaiʻi
She is as lovely as the morning dawn,
  This Princess, flower of our beloved land.

Wonderful news comes of your achievement.
  Word of it spreads to all Honolulu.
We laud your success, dear Kaʻiulani,
  In restoring our Queen to her throne.
And, "Ua mau e ka ea o ka ʻAina."
  We say, prayerfully and in unison,
"Long may the flag of Hawaiʻi fly!"
  We cry it . . . so the world may hear.

We cry it, hearts overflowing with love,
  For we are deeply grateful, Kaʻiulani.
You have won all, with your charm and beauty.
  Kaʻiulani, you have captured every heart!

Lovely niece of our beloved Queen
  Aliʻi, successor to her throne
You are ours, our lovely Royal Princess
  And deep is the love Hawaiʻi bears you.
Thus ends my song, a song of tribute,
  A song in praise of lovely Kaʻiulani!

Realizing that their princess was now a young woman, the citizens of Honolulu found themselves speculating not only about her political accomplishments but also about her romantic life. Since Koa was back and obviously not engaged, the only other young man on the scene — and therefore the only other obvious candidate — was Theo Davies' son Clive, whom Ka'iulani and the Davies had visited in Boston.

One anti-Royalist paper, hinting that Ka'iulani was slighting native Hawaiians, actually reported that Clive and Ka'iulani were engaged. Archie vehemently denied that his daughter was involved with anyone.

The Hawaiians didn't know that at that time, another romantic possibility for Ka'iulani was of more interest to Queen Lili'uokalani.

England wasn't the only nation that didn't want the United States to claim the Hawaiian Islands. Since the end of February, the *Naniwa*, a Japanese naval cruiser, had been anchored off O'ahu. Lili'uokalani knew something about the Japanese that Ka'iulani did not yet know.

When King Kalākaua had made his world tour, he had been impressed with the military might of Japan. He saw an alliance with Japan as a way that Hawai'i could stand up to Western pressure.

While visiting a Japanese naval academy, Kalākaua had been favorably impressed by a young Japanese prince named Komatsu. During a private meeting with the Japanese emperor, Kalākaua had proposed an arranged marriage between Komatsu and Ka'iulani.

At the time, the offer was neither accepted nor rejected. Komatsu himself had written Kalākaua, formally thanking him but saying that a marriage had already been arranged for him when he was very young. He implied, however, that engagements can sometimes be broken.

Events in Hawai'i since then had not lent themselves to further discussions with Japan.

Now, however, Queen Lili'uokalani was informed that Prince Komatsu himself was on board the *Naniwa*. His presence — and Japan's interest in the situation — seemed too intentional to be coincidental.

Could Kaʻiulani help the Islands regain their sovereignty in another way?

There were so many positive signs about the queen's possible restoration that Liliʻuokalani wasn't yet ready to throw off the yoke of one larger nation only to be shackled to another. Still, joining forces with Japan was a possibility.

But Liliʻuokalani's immediate thoughts concerning her niece were troubling ones. As much as she loved Kaʻiulani, the princess's immense popularity, combined with Liliʻuokalani's own turbulent situation, made the possibility that Kaʻiulani would replace Liliʻuokalani a very real one.

In England, Kaʻiulani received a letter from her aunt, dated May 24. The queen began by commenting that work was going well on the new residence at ʻĀinahau, but that Archie looked a little thin. Then she said,

> I would simply like to add and say that should anyone write or propose or make any proposition to you in any way in regard to taking the Throne, I hope you will be guarded in your answer. The people all over the Islands have petitioned to have me restored and it would make you appear in an awkward light to accept any overtures from any irresponsible party, and the PGs are growing less and less, and I understand they will soon drop to pieces as the saying is, for want of funds to carry the Government. . . . We are waiting patiently until the US Commissioner in Mr. Stevens' place [can] tell us we are free. I will write you and acquaint you of all that transpires, and if need be will advise you after consulting with your father.

Kaʻiulani put down the letter, her head spinning. Once again she felt she was living a double life! She might be the toast of Ho-

The executive council of the Provisional Government
(l. to r. James A. King, Sanford B. Dole, William O. Smith, Peter C. Jones)

nolulu, according to gossip practically married and about to ascend the throne — but in reality, she was lonely and poor, relying on the good graces of her former schoolmistress, with whom she shared a little house in Kettering. (Since the overthrow, the P.G.s had completely cut off Kaʻiulani's educational stipend. She and her father had agreed that she would have to live on only five hundred pounds a year until things were settled and she could come home.)

Forgoing polite language and forced cheerfulness, Kaʻiulani wrote to her aunt, explaining exactly how she felt:

I have never received any proposals from anybody to take the Throne. I have not received a word of any sort from anyone except

141

my father. I am glad that I am able to say that I have not written to anyone about politics.

I have been perfectly miserable during the past four months. I have looked forward to '93 as being the end of my "exile." I have considered the last four years I have been in England as years of exile. Now it seems as though things [will] never settle and I am simply longing to see you all. . . .

I am staying with my old school mistress Mrs. Sharp. She gave up her school two years ago, and is now living in a dear little home of her own.

I am as happy as I can possibly be under the circumstances. I am really and truly recruiting my health which has not been good lately. I do a good deal of hard reading, practicing, sewing and gardening. I am getting to be quite a good needle-woman. . . .

I will try to be cheerful, but I am so homesick!

How Kaʻiulani longed to be back in Oʻahu, in the thick of things, helping Auntie! Hadn't she proved her loyalty and ability in Washington? Yet here she was in a "dear little home" far away, sewing and gardening. The frustration was nearly unbearable.

While they waited for Commissioner Blount to make his report, the Davies invited Kaʻiulani to summer with them in a rented house in Killeny, outside of Dublin, Ireland. Although the P.G.s had stripped ʻIolani Palace and were using it as their headquarters, Mr. Davies had hopes that justice would be done.

Kaʻiulani did her best to enjoy the summer. A group of sixteen young men and women were staying at the house, several of them her old friends. (Certainly seeing Clive was awkward at first, but the two were soon able to laugh about their fabricated engagement.) They had frequent picnics and nonstop games of tennis. And yet the future of a nation . . . and of a young woman . . . was being decided so far away.

"Paramount Blount" with his wife (above) and in a cartoon in which he oversees
the lowering of the U.S. flag in Hawai'i (below)

*   *   *

WHEN JAMES BLOUNT left Hawaiʻi in August, hopes were high for restoration.

In fact, Blount's report stated unequivocally that a great wrong had been done to the Hawaiian people and that full sovereignty should be restored. But because President Cleveland was in poor health, a new American minister did not arrive in Honolulu with instructions until November. Those were long months in Hawaiʻi. Tensions ran deep, and the economy was near collapse because no one was certain which government would end up in control.

*   *   *

KAʻIULANI RETURNED TO Mrs. Sharp's home in autumn, but not for long. The Davies invited the princess to join their daughter Alice and three other friends on a winter trip to Germany, to study the culture and perfect their German. Kaʻiulani decided to look on this as an abbreviated version of her long-postponed "tour" of the Continent, hoping good news would finally call her home to Hawaiʻi at its completion.

In October, the princess spent her eighteenth birthday not at ʻĀinahau as planned but in London at a celebration given by Hawaiian friends abroad. Back home, Liliʻuokalani hosted a giant party in Kaʻiulani's honor at Washington Place. Again, the double life: all Kaʻiulani could do was read about her party — all the gifts of love she had received, the crowds who had attended, and the band that had played all day on the lānai specially constructed for the occasion.

*   *   *

Albert Willis, the new
American minister
to Hawaiʻi

IN NOVEMBER, THE new American minister, Albert Willis, arrived in Honolulu. In a private meeting with Liliʻuokalani, he informed her that President Cleveland agreed with James Blount that
a great wrong had been done to Hawaiʻi. His instructions were to re-
instate the monarchy — on the condition that the men involved in
the overthrow be granted full pardon.

Liliʻuokalani felt strongly that if the P.G.s were pardoned, the
situation would remain essentially unchanged: they would fight her
authority and cause trouble at every turn.

No, she said, amnesty was impossible. According to Willis's report,

145

she planned on having the perpetrators beheaded and their property confiscated. Later, she would deny she had ever urged beheading; but whatever her position, it shocked Willis enough that instead of going ahead with the restoration, he decided to return to Washington to report the queen's position and wait for further instructions.

During November, the P.G.s got word about the planned reinstatement, and they began arming themselves. In addition, a new U.S. warship arrived in the harbor. Although the commander of this ship was under instructions to help restore the queen, he dreaded giving the order for his Marines to open fire on the P.G.s, who were, after all, American citizens. The P.G.s, however, had come to the conclusion that they were perfectly willing to fire on the U.S. Marines.

When Willis returned to Hawaiʻi in December, he came with the same offer: total amnesty in return for restoration. On December 16, the queen said absolutely not. Her final offer was to banish her enemies and sell their property to pay the country's debts.

On December 19, realizing that Cleveland's position was firm and responding to the urging of her advisors, she finally agreed to amnesty. But by then it was too late. When Willis called on Sanford Dole to tell him that President Cleveland was ordering the P.G.s to step down, they were ready with their answer: No.

All Willis could do with this answer was cable it to Washington and wait for instructions.

Realizing that annexation was hopeless under Cleveland, the P.G.s declared themselves no longer American citizens with any allegiance to the U.S. president. The Royalists, meanwhile, were sure that the United States would back up its decision with force. The tense standoff continued.

*   *   *

HALF A WORLD away, Ka'iulani was trying to distract herself in Germany. She had attended a parade of 20,000 soldiers before the emperor and empress in Berlin — and she had caught the attention of a dashing German count. He was extremely well-to-do, and he enjoyed showing her his country. Ka'iulani had to admit it was great fun, for once, to enjoy herself without worrying about money. However, when the count proposed marriage, she had to admit to him that she did not reciprocate his feelings.

But that got her thinking. She had wondered — knowing that so many fabrications had been interwoven in the newspaper stories — whether the queen really had any plans concerning herself and Prince Koa. So she wrote and asked.

The queen's answer, written at the end of January 1894, caught her completely by surprise.

> My Dear Niece,
>
> Your father called the other day and kindly handed me your note, and I am so glad to hear from you. It is true that many reports have been circulated in the newspapers about my restoration, and in fact, many thought it was already settled, but many causes arose which prevented its immediate accomplishment, but I suppose you will have read of it by this time and everything connected with our situation by the President's Message to the Senate and Congress. The delay is unfortunate, but the President has said the wrong must be righted, and so it will have to be according to my protest. . . . So my dear child we are only waiting for the "good news," then you may come home. It has been weary waiting. . . . Business has been dull, no money circulating and those who have it will not spend because of the present government — as everything done now is illegal. . . .
>
> You have asked me a direct question and I must be candid

Kaʻiulani felt increasingly melancholy as her hopes for homecoming were repeatedly dashed.

with you in regard to Prince David. I had not thought of mentioning to you about your future until the proper moment arrived but as you already mention it, it is best you should marry one or the other of the Princes, that we may have more aliʻi. There are no other aliʻi whom they (the people) look to except Prince David or his brother who would be eligible to the Throne, or worthy of it, and they turn to these two aliʻi that there may be more aliʻi to make the Throne permanent according to the Constitution. To you then depends the hope of the nation and unfortunately we cannot always do as we like, in our position as ruler and which

148

you will have to be some day. In some things our course and actions will have to be guided by certain rules . . . which could not be avoided. I am pleased to see your candor in regard to Prince David — it is good to be candid.

I have to mention another matter, one which I think you ought to know and I hope you will write at your earliest chance and inform me what your opinion is in this matter. When your uncle, the late King, was living, he made arrangements that you should be united to one of the Japanese Princes. He is the nephew to the Emperor of Japan. It seems that the young Prince was here in the *Naniwa* on her first trip last year, but our position was such that he could not present himself, so I have not seen him. I understand now that the Prince is in England being educated so you may meet him on your return. I do not know his name but should you meet him and think you could like him I give you full leave to accept him, should he propose to you and offer his hand and fortune. It would be a good alliance. They speak highly of his qualities. And now do not hesitate to open your heart to me. I shall be very glad if such an alliance could be consummated between you two and I shall look forward to a letter from you with eagerness, saying it was agreeable to you, and that you will encourage his suit.

While Kaʻiulani had almost expected the answer about Koa and Kūhiō, she was stunned by her aunt's strong urging that she marry Prince Komatsu. It seemed, in fact, that Liliʻuokalani was more eager for Kaʻiulani to marry the Japanese prince than the Hawaiian aliʻi. This was not only surprising news; it betrayed the queen's fear that restoration might not go smoothly and an alliance with another strong nation had become not only expedient but immediately desirable.

Was it true? Did Kaʻiulani's position dictate that she must marry someone from another country, someone she'd never even met, to save her nation?

Her mother's prophecy about her marriage (or lack thereof) was one thing; in her strongest moments, she could write it off as superstition. But her aunt's request and the plight of Hawaiʻi were undeniably real. Must she marry out of duty?

Her aunt had closed the letter by swearing her to secrecy, so she couldn't even discuss the matter with the Davies!

Normally she answered the queen's letters immediately upon receiving them. This time, she couldn't bring herself to answer for a long time.

In Berlin, on June 10, she answered a letter of her father's, in which he reported that the P.G.s were trying to make Hawaiʻi an independent nation under their control. She wrote,

> What a dreadful state our Hawaiʻi nei is in. I simply cry when I think over things. It will never be the same again to any of us. If things come to the worst, you will have to come here and stay here in Europe. We could find out a quiet spot where the climate suits you and there we should live.
>
> My dearest you cannot possibly think we could go home and live there, if there is a republic, just think of the insults we should receive from the [P.G.s] who were once under us. No I could not stand it!

Two weeks later, when she was back in England, Kaʻiulani finally found her voice to answer the queen:

Dearest Aunt,
It is a very long time since I received your kind letter. I have often

tried to answer it, but have failed. I have thought over what you said in it about my marrying some Prince from Japan.

Unless it is absolutely necessary, I would much rather not do so.

I could have married an enormously rich German Count, but I could not care for him. I feel it would be wrong if I married a man I did not love. I should be perfectly unhappy, and we should not agree and instead of being an example to the married women of today, I should become like them, merely a woman of fashion and most likely a flirt. I hope I am not expressing myself too strongly, but I feel I must speak out to you and there must be perfect confidence between you and me dear Aunt.

I have been looking anxiously every day in the papers for news from home, but nothing seems to have happened. I wish things could be properly settled. It is such weary work waiting here not knowing what is happening.

Weary work indeed. Her whole life was at a standstill. Again she spent the summer with the Davies in Ireland. Occasionally she tried to imagine that she was just another young woman summering with them, that her greatest goal was making a suitable marriage and running a happy home. But the thought of what would make her own marriage "suitable" brought those musings to an abrupt halt.

More often, she wondered whether, if worse came to worst, she could face a life of permanent exile, away from her beloved Hawai'i. She fervently hoped it wouldn't come to that.

*   *   *

KA'IULANI'S NEXT BAD news came shortly after July 4. Many U.S. congressmen had been vocally against President Cleveland's attempt

Sanford Dole proclaims Hawai'i a republic on July 4, 1894.

to restore Hawai'i's queen. One U.S. paper had roared, "Native rule, ignorant, naked, heathen, is re-established." Cleveland did not have the political backing to militarily unseat the P.G.s.

The newspaper that Ka'iulani and the Davies read on that July morning told the story: In Hawai'i, the P.G.s had held a vote, "ratifying" a republic. Of approximately 150,000 Hawaiian residents, fewer than 800 had been allowed to vote. The P.G.s had turned themselves into a sovereign nation: the Republic of Hawai'i. They celebrated the "new" nation on July 4.

"It'll never last!" cried Clive. "The P.G.s — sorry, the Republicans — are wildly unpopular. They didn't even dare risk a popular vote!"

"I predict they won't last past Christmas," said Mr. Davies.

It was Mrs. Davies who saw how deeply stricken the princess was. "It will be cleared up by Christmas," she said hopefully to Ka'iulani. "We'd be honored to have you stay with us until then."

"They'll get no backing from the U.S. — from anyone!" sputtered Mr. Davies.

It seemed at first that Mr. Davies was correct. President Cleveland asked Congress for a solution "consistent with honor, integrity, morality." But in August, the U.S. Congress recognized the Republic of Hawai'i.

President Cleveland felt forced to do the same.

Ka'iulani felt each action as a betrayal. Grover Cleveland — who'd promised her justice, who'd welcomed her as a friend!

The princess began to suffer frequent, debilitating headaches.

"Honor, integrity, morality" — they didn't seem to stand a chance.

Her royal highness Victoria Ka'iulani — a princess still in exile

TEN

Exile

During the fall of 1894, Kaʻiulani again helped Alice Davies raise funds for charity, this time at a bazaar. Kaʻiulani herself won two prizes — one of which was a St. Bernard puppy! It was the sort of unexpected silliness that couldn't help but cheer her from time to time. That Christmas was her sixth far from home. At nineteen, she had been away from the land that defined her for almost a third of her life.

In January, she returned to Rozel, Jersey, at the invitation of her old mentor, Mrs. Rooke. She loved the steep hills and swooping birds of this small island. It was here, in a gentler, quieter atmosphere, that she felt a tranquility deeper than in any other place outside Hawaiʻi.

Sadly, it was here, toward the end of the month, that she got more bad news. The Royalists had struck back in a counter-revolution — but it had failed.

After the main force had been defeated at the base of Diamond

Prince Kūhiō wearing a
prisoner's stripes

Head, the Republicans (as the P.G.s were now known) had lashed
out in anger, jailing more than two hundred known Royalists, including Aunt Liliʻuokalani and princes Koa and Kūhiō.

In a turnaround on Liliʻuokalani's alleged wish for "beheading," the Republicans threatened death, on grounds of treason, to
those who had taken part in the failed coup unless Liliʻuokalani
signed a paper abdicating the throne once and for all. To spare the
lives of loyal subjects, she agreed to sign.

The Republicans put the former queen on trial in what had

been the throne room of 'Iolani Palace. Trying to regain her rights had become an act of treason. She was found guilty and sentenced to five years' hard labor and fined five thousand dollars. Although this part of the sentence was not carried out, the former queen was immediately imprisoned in an upstairs bedroom of the palace.

Ka'iulani was stricken to the core that this "band of hooligans" (as Mr. Davies had called them) had the arrogance and audacity to treat Lili'uokalani in such a disrespectful and mean-spirited way. This terrible occurrence also meant that there was no way Ka'iulani could return home now, when the atmosphere was so dangerous for royals.

In fact, her father found the situation so oppressive that he left O'ahu in July to join Ka'iulani.

Archie arrived at the Davies' place, where Ka'iulani was again summering, on August 10. Ka'iulani was tremendously happy to see him. As demanding and irritating as he could be (father and daughter still had explosive arguments), he was completely devoted to her, and she to him. She had been a solitary figure for so long that it was wonderful to again be part of a pair.

Just after the overthrow, Archie had felt Ka'iulani might be happier if she returned to Hawai'i and lived a private life as a woman of tremendous influence — as had Mrs. Berneice Bishop (who had once refused the throne) and several other high ali'i women. Now he was so deeply hurt by the bitter accusations and lies printed by the Republicans that Ka'iulani's idea of living permanently in Europe sounded like a possibility.

"But things are far from settled back home," he told her. "Many, many people, even non-Hawaiians, are sick and tired of the Republicans' oppressive rule. It's an open secret that most of the men in power know that their Republic isn't strong enough to last. They're only trying to hold on until Cleveland is out of office in hopes that annexation will be considered again." He lowered his voice. "But many hold out hope for a return to a fair and just constitutional monarchy. And you remain the hope of the Hawaiian people. There's even an organization called ʻIndependent Americans for Kaʻiulani.' It helps that you've been so far away during all this trouble. You can't be blamed for anything, even by the Republicans — though Lord knows, they still try!"

On September 7, Liliʻuokalani was released from her "prison" at the palace but remained under house arrest at Washington Place. Prince Kūhiō was also released from the Oʻahu prison called "The Reef." Within a few weeks he married a Hawaiian aliʻi who had visited him often during his imprisonment. (Koa had been jailed only briefly.)

Archie and Kaʻiulani visited Scotland, then decided to winter on the French Riviera. They rented a home called the Villa du Cap in the charming town of Menton. Many other society people from Britain and the Continent were also there.

It was here Kaʻiulani realized that if she spent every day worrying about the situation in Hawaiʻi, she'd go mad. Right now there was no action she could take to help things. Instead, she decided to concentrate on her life in the present — on the happiness she found in the company of her father and good friends.

In many ways she would succeed. Yet friends' descriptions of her from that time, while they began with words like "witty," "charming," and "vivacious," always seemed to end with the mention of "an underlying sadness in her eyes."

At Menton, it was easy to live in the present. Here, she was not treated like *former* royalty at all but like the crown princess of Hawaiʻi. She and her father were in the midst of a happy social whirl, often attending dinners and dances given at fashionable homes. On these occasions, Kaʻiulani wore her beautiful gowns, ac-

Queen Liliʻuokalani in her front room (above) and outside her
home at Washington Place (below)

cepted bows and curtsies with a smile, and was again addressed as "Your Highness." When she was alone in her rooms, troubling thoughts might come tiptoeing back, but when she was on the dance floor, being whirled in a waltz, nothing mattered but the guiding hand of her partner, the swirl of dresses, and the rise and fall of the music.

On the Riviera, Kaʻiulani easily made friends with both young women and young men, including a small circle with whom she became very close. One of these intimates was an English baron named Nevinson de Courcy — or Toby, as he was nicknamed. A hundred years later, writer Kristin Zambucka discovered that the letters written by the princess to the young baron had been preserved all that time by his family. Much of Kaʻiulani's spirit comes through in her words.

One cheerful note says,

My Dear Toby,
Very many thanks for your [letter] of the 28th. I also heard from Sib that she had seen you — you both say the other was looking very pale and thin. Mon Ami qu est ce qu'il-y-a? Surely you are not ailing! And I trust above all things you are not suffering from mal au coeur [a broken heart]. I have been very seedy. Papa was over in town so he consulted the Dr. I have been suffering from too much worry!!! So I am to sleep a great deal etc. Evidently dancing is not harmful otherwise Papa would have prevented my going to a dance on Wednesday. Toby I feel so naughty, I have such a nice flirtation on pour le moment. Don't be shocked, and leave your lecture until we meet in Menton — it is too good to believe that I shall have the pleasure of seeing you soon — won't we talk! I have such piles to tell you. I have Gertie Somers staying with me and also a Miss Brander — we are about the three biggest

Kaʻiulani's friend
Toby de Courcy

flirts you could find, so we simply have a lovely time. Just fancy Pa went to London on Tuesday last and returned yesterday. We had quite a nice time by ourselves!!!

It is a relief to find her sounding like a normal young woman enjoying her friends and her flirtations. The only hint of other concerns — that when in Hawaiʻi, Theo Davies had been forced to quell rumors and publicly deny that Kaʻiulani had military designs on the throne — is her almost careless reference to feeling "seedy" and being diagnosed with "too much worry."

Kaʻiulani and her father moved from Menton in the winter to Paris in the spring, then back to England and Scotland for the summer and fall. In Paris, Kaʻiulani was once again treated like royalty. She attended the famous Bazar de Charité on its opening day.

In the fall of 1896, Kaʻiulani wrote to Toby about a very interesting matter. Happy to be back in Rozel (the island town where she'd stayed before with Mrs. Rooke), she said,

At last we got back to our little Jersey home. I was quite glad to get back though the trees are all bare, and the weather far from nice — still, it is the one place that I can boss the show, so to speak. I am feeling very dull indeed. Papa has a bad cold, and is consequently in the vilest of tempers. It is most unfortunate as he has been free from colds for so long. He has an idea that he is going to pip which is most annoying — however one must put up with these little annoyances.

We spent a week in [London], and then stayed a week with some friends at Southsea. I saw the "Prisoner of Zenda" and "A Night Out" whilst in town — I simply howled with laughter at the latter — it was really too funny. . . . We were pretty gay at the Langham — had a charming suite of rooms, and simply went the pace while we were up. . . .

One of my young men came out to see me yesterday — I am supposed to be polishing him off — I can't make up my mind to do so just yet, must have a little more fun as my fling is limited — I intend to get as much amusement this winter as I possibly can. There is a possibility of my being married in April to a man I don't care much for either way — rather a gloomy outlook — but "noblesse oblige" — I must have been born under an unlucky star — as I seem to have my life planned out for me in such a way that I cannot alter it. . . .

My engagement is a "great secret" — approved of by Mr. Davies and my Father — it is being kept secret for political reasons.

Since no engagement was ever announced, history does not tell us for certain who the gentleman in question was. But if Ka'iulani agreed to marry for political reasons, it could only be to help her Hawaiian people. And, as her aunt had written, the way to do that was to marry another high ali'i — and Koa was the only one of the two princes suggested by Lili'uokalani who was still available.

If her intended was David Kawānanakoa, however, it is likely that, despite the protest in her letter, both she and Koa had very strong — and very conflicted — feelings about each other. They were both passionate, attractive, powerful people who shared a role in history, who had been close at one time. However, both had hurt each other publicly and politically: Ka'iulani by taking the governorship of O'ahu from Koa and snubbing him in Washington; Koa by speaking against Ka'iulani to the Washington press. It is little wonder that their feelings were ambivalent.

But Ka'iulani and Koa united — the heir apparent wed to the heir presumptive — would be a strong rallying point for Hawaiian nationals. And there was nothing the Republicans could do to outlaw such a marriage.

* * *

AS SOON AS Lili'uokalani was released from house arrest at Washington Place in January of 1897, she left for Washington, D.C., to take her cause directly to the seat of U.S. government and to the new president, William McKinley, who was rumored to favor expansionism — gaining as much territory as possible.

President William McKinley, proponent of American expansion

Kaʻiulani, although "hoping to have a pleasant winter" with Toby and her friends, became ill in Menton. She had a severe bout with "la grippe" (the flu), which had plagued her repeatedly since the overthrow. She wrote to her aunt, asking permission to return to Hawaiʻi, but was refused.

Eventually Kaʻiulani and her father grew tired of their wandering. They decided to move to Paris in early April and stay there indefinitely. Kaʻiulani understood her father's desire to settle down and to stop imposing on the kindness of friends such as the Davies. However, the thought of calling Paris home — calling any place besides the Islands home — was almost more than she could bear.

"Once the social season begins, with the Bazar de Charité, you'll feel a part of things," Archie had said in an attempt to console her.

But in March they got shocking news that neither had expected. Annie, Archie's daughter and Kaʻiulani's half-sister and best friend, died suddenly at age twenty-nine.

Both Archie and Kaʻiulani were staggered by the loss. Kaʻiulani was fighting so hard to get back to Hawaiʻi — but there were fewer and fewer loved ones who would be there to greet her when she returned.

*   *   *

WHEN IT CAME time to move to Paris from Menton, Archie was too ill to travel, but Kaʻiulani went on ahead with a chaperone, according to plans. They moved into their apartment at 37 Avenue Marceau, Champs Elysées. While Kaʻiulani waited for her father to join her, she became friends with the family in the next apartment: a count and his two daughters, who were near her age. All of them received coveted invitations to the opening afternoon of that year's

The town of Menton, where Ka'iulani was treated like royalty

Grand Bazaar. For the festivities, an area adjoining the Hotel du Palais would be walled in, covered over, and transformed into an "old-fashioned" street of Paris. This event was considered the beginning of the Paris social season; all the royalty and socially elite would attend.

Ka'iulani tried to be excited about the gala, but it was getting harder and harder for her not to be absorbed by the great sadness of Annie's death and her continuing exile.

Archie arrived in Paris in time for the Grand Bazaar. Her gown chosen and pressed, the arrangements made, Ka'iulani awoke the morning of the gala with one of her debilitating migraine headaches. She was unable even to sit up. Her father immediately called for the doctor, who informed her that she was going nowhere that day.

It was a headache that saved her life.

For at the height of the afternoon's festivities, a fire started in the cinematograph, a small theater that had been set up. Within minutes, it swept over the wooden roof covering the Grand Bazaar. The wooden walls became flaming barriers; the attendees were trapped as if inside a burning wooden box. Over one hundred people died.

The next week, on May 9, 1897, Ka'iulani wrote to her aunt on the black-bordered stationery she'd used since Annie's death:

My Dear Aunt,
Very many thanks for your kind letter.

Annie's sudden death has been a very great shock to both of us — I can hardly realise that the dear girl has gone.

I am sorry to say I am not feeling at all well.

My nerves are all out of order and I suffer continually from headaches.

I daresay you have already heard of the awful catastrophe which took place here at the Bazar de Charité. I have never heard of anything so fearful in my life. Nearly all of the 117 victims were women and young ones too. There is a count next door who has lost his two daughters, girls of 18 and 19.

What strikes one so is it's being in one's own station of life, the smartest society women of Paris.

The death of the Duchesse d'Alemon throws the Austrian, Belgian and Bavarian Courts into mourning, not counting the Arleans and King of Naples families. Just imagine all those people gone in less than half an hour. And the dreadful agony they must have suffered. I have never seen any place so overcast as the gay City of Paris — you see all the people selling were connected with the highest aristocracy of France.

I hope that you are keeping well and that you are enjoying yourself in Washington. I am going on the 18th to Ravensdale, Tunbridge Wells to stay with the Davies. I hope the change will do me some good.

The idea of living in Paris was abandoned for good.

*   *   *

AFTER VISITING THE Davies, Ka'iulani and her father returned in July to the island of Jersey. From there she wrote to her friend Toby:

I am really feeling much better, but have still to be very careful. I was so annoyed a few days back. I managed to get down for breakfast and stayed up fairly late in the evening, having also played croquet during the afternoon, when on my way to bed, I again had one of my fainting fits. It showed me that I must be more careful, but all the same it is very hard lines, and I hate posing as an invalid.

Where are you going to spend your Summer? There is some talk of my going over to pay my revered Aunt a visit, but as yet things are extremely undecided. They talk of Annexation, but whether they will get it is quite another thing. However, things are in a very bad way out there, and I am now pretty certain that we shall never have back our own again. . . . I am really rather sorry the way the whole thing has finished up, much better [to] have a republic than to lose our nationality altogether. . . . I am very sorry for my people, as they will hate being taken over by another nation.

If I went over to see my Aunt I would only stay about three

weeks and then return here again. My ex-Guardian is going out to Hawai'i the latter part of September. He has a great deal of interest in sugar, and he seems anxious about it. He may think it advisable for me to return home the end of this Winter.

Theo Davies wasn't the only one who wanted Ka'iulani to return to Hawai'i. Someone forwarded to her and her father a copy of the Hawaiian newspaper *The Independent,* dated June 28. It ran a letter that had been sent to Washington by a prominent American businessman. He talked about how he believed in democracy, but also commented,

Living under a mythical republic composed merely of its office holders . . . a minority upheld by force of arms . . . [has led to] intense disgust and hostility against the present absurd methods of government. And that is the situation as it exists in Hawai'i today; apathy, disgust, and hostility.

Now . . . after this, what? There is no standard around which to rally. . . . Give our longings and aspirations a concrete form, send for your Ka'iulani, let her after a reasonable sojourn among the American people, during which they may discover for themselves her true worth, her fitness for the position of Queen over the Hawaiian people, return to the land of her birth, once more to take up her residence . . . to quietly and confidently bide the time when the indignant protests of all right-minded, self-respecting citizens against this . . . travesty called a republic shall have swept it out of existence. . . .

I hold that the decision [about annexation] rests with the Hawaiians; that so long as they, the children of the soil, intelligent citizens, decline to take that view, the United States will take no steps toward Annexation [nor] accede to the ridiculous pretensions of a minority whose motive is . . . merely one of self interest.

. . . That is why I am for Kaʻiulani, and why the slight influence it is my good fortune to be able to wield . . . is cast in her favor, and why the large majority of foreigners — Americans, British, Portuguese — will support the same sentiment at the proper time.

As honored as Kaʻiulani was by this demonstration of public sentiment, part of her wondered if the struggle would ever end. There had been so much back-and-forth — hope given, hope taken away. Living in a state of not knowing for five long years was taking its toll. She had to act as though the cause were lost, yet be in a position to assume leadership when the call came.

*　　*　　*

FOR KAʻIULANI, THE call came in June, when President McKinley resubmitted the Annexation Treaty to Congress.

Kaʻiulani and her father discussed the situation late into the night. Kaʻiulani felt the Hawaiians would need a leader and a role model, whichever way things went.

She knew Liliʻuokalani did not want her to go home. But Kaʻiulani, who had been a loyal niece for so long, finally rebelled. She could no longer live a double life. Her life *was* Hawaiʻi and the Hawaiian people. There was nothing for her in Europe. A life in "high society" might be fine for others, but, as Theo Davies had said, she saw it as her goal to serve the King of Kings. And her place of service was clearly with her people. Whatever the future held for her Islands, she wanted to be there to help.

"Papa, I'm going home," she announced firmly at the end of their discussion.

Archie covered her small hand with his own. This exile had

drained him, and he'd been gone for only two years, not eight. "It's time, Daughter," he said. "It's time."

Princess Kaʻiulani in San Francisco — finally on her way back home

ELEVEN

Home at Last

Ka'iulani found it harder than she expected to pack up eight years of life — and to find an English maid willing to travel to Hawai'i who didn't request an astronomical amount of money.

Yet she finally was acting with a keen sense of purpose. She was going home, returning to her people. Her exile was over.

The Cleghorns made farewell calls on the loyal friends and supporters who had meant so much to the princess over the years. But when the *Paris* sailed from its berth in Southampton on October 9, Ka'iulani looked forward, with faith, to her destiny.

Again, reports of her in the New York press were glowing. Ironically, however, she was upstaged by another young woman, Evangelina Cosalo y Cisneros. The senorita had recently tried to free her country, Cuba, from a tyrannical government by trying to assassinate one of the oppressors. She had escaped jail with the aid of an American reporter; now New York was having a huge rally in her honor.

Liliʻuokalani in
Washington, D.C., where
she was opposing the
Annexation Treaty

Kaʻiulani couldn't help but wonder — Had acting with dignity
and counting on justice gone out of fashion? Would the Americans
find her more heroic if she had she picked up a gun and urged others to do the same?

The fact was, it didn't matter what others thought. Kaʻiulani
knew her only judges were God and her people. She would continue
to act in a way she thought honored them.

It was with both eagerness and apprehension that she prepared
to visit her Aunt Liliʻuokalani, who was staying at the Ebbett House
in Washington, D.C. The former queen had come to make swift ob-

jection to the resubmission of the Annexation Treaty; she was also working on writing the story of her life and the overthrow of her government.

Ka'iulani was returning to Hawai'i without her aunt's permission. And yet, as politically wary of Ka'iulani as Lili'uokalani was, the two had become very close through their frequent letters to each other.

When the two women, one older and rotund, the other young and slim, finally met again face to face, they fell into each other's arms. Let politics intrude at another time; at this moment, they were aunt and niece, the last remaining members of an illustrious, close-knit family. They had both endured much and lost much. When they talked, it was about their family, and they spoke from the heart.

Seeing her niece in person, Lili'uokalani was impressed. She saw that Ka'iulani had matured into a wise, thoughtful young woman. What a great team they might have made, sharing as they did a similar devotion to their people and their God.

But it was clear to Archie that the extreme difficulties which Lili'uokalani had endured — the stolen throne, the mock trial, the enforced imprisonment, the threats on her life — had made her bitter, while Ka'iulani, despite her struggles, was not. Perhaps it was a good thing that his daughter had been kept so far from the turmoil at home.

The Cleghorns' visit to Washington was brief. As soon as they could, they boarded the train for the long ride from Washington to San Francisco. Once there, they registered at the Occidental Hotel as simply "A. S. Cleghorn, daughter and maid."

But with all the dinners and entertainments planned in Ka'iulani's honor, it wasn't long before the whole city knew they were staying there. Archie told reporters who clamored for stories, "My daughter will be pleased to see you. But not to talk politics."

The reporter from *The Examiner* had heard the Republicans' continued claims that the Hawaiians were savages, and he couldn't refute this strongly enough:

A barbarian princess? Not a bit of it. Not even a hemi-semi-demi barbarian. Rather the very flower — an exotic — of civilization. The Princess Kaʻiulani is a charming, fascinating individual. She has the taste and style of a French woman; the admirable repose and soft voice of an English woman. She was gowned for dinner in a soft, black, high-necked frock, with the latest Parisian touches in every fold. . . . She is tall, of willowy slenderness, erect and graceful, with a small, pale face, full red lips, soft expression, dark eyes, a very good nose, and a cloud of crimpy black hair knotted high.

Again, as she had years before, Kaʻiulani sat for a portrait — in the very gown described in *The Examiner*. Again her dress was black, but this time it clothed a statelier, infinitely wiser young woman. Reporters were impressed by both her beauty and her gentle wisdom, as evidenced by the description of her in *The Call*:

She is beautiful. . . . There is no portrait that does justice to her expressive, small, proud face. She is exquisitely slender and graceful, holds herself like a princess, like a Hawaiian — and I know of no simile more descriptive of grace and dignity than this last. . . . Her accent says London; her figure says New York; her heart says Hawaiʻi. . . . But she is more than a beautiful pretender to an abdicated throne. . . . She has been made a woman of the world by the life she has led.

The final sea passage to the Islands on the *Australia* was made especially interesting by the fact that a number of the passengers belonged to a respected theater company traveling to perform in Honolulu. Yet Ka'iulani's anticipation of reaching her homeland overshadowed everything else.

*   *   *

NOVEMBER 9, 1897, was sunny and clear. From afar, the Islands looked just as Ka'iulani remembered them, their lush greenery rising from the warm, briny waves to greet her. There was Moloka'i, and there, rising dramatically, was Diamond Head, marking the nearness of Waikīkī — 'Āinahau — home.

In many ways, her arrival mirrored her departure years ago. As the ship approached the docks below Honolulu, Ka'iulani and her father could see the teeming crowds waiting excitedly to see their princess. Again the band was playing, thousands of people waved their welcome, and the air was fragrant with flowers.

And yet she wasn't returning, as she had dreamed of doing, with unfettered joy. Her heart held both deep joy and deep sorrow, each threatening to engulf the other at any moment.

Family and friends swarmed aboard the ship to greet their princess. By the time she again set foot on Hawaiian soil, she was covered with dozens of lei.

Prince Koa and Eva Parker accompanied the Cleghorns in their carriage. Ka'iulani was tremendously touched by the tears of joy — and perhaps, of new hope? — wept by many in the crowds. As mothers and fathers held their children up to get a look at the princess, Ka'iulani realized with a shock that none of these *keiki* had even been born when she'd left eight-and-a-half years ago. She had been nothing but a story to them.

The new house at 'Āinahau had been built for a queen. The

The new house at ʻĀinahau, which Archie had completed for
Kaʻiulani's homecoming in late 1897

lāanai were long and wide. An elegant reception room ran the
length of the house; a parlor and a comfortable, informal "mosquito
room" completed the public rooms on the first floor. Upstairs,
Kaʻiulani's bedroom was flanked by a sitting room and a dressing
room; the ceilings had repeated patterns of kāhilis and coronets, the
symbols of Hawaiian royalty.

The house was beautiful and stately, but again Kaʻiulani felt
pain mixed with pleasure. Each room bespoke the position which, it
seemed, would never be hers.

Kaʻiulani also became wistful when she made a private visit to
the mausoleum at Nuʻuanu, where King Kalākaua now rested near

Mama. The trip there and back proved how much had changed. New buildings, new faces . . . so much was different. She could not bring herself to even look at the palace, now the executive building of the "Republic."

But those first days of her return brought happiness as well. Whenever she could, she wore loose holokū. She fed her peacocks, and she rode her beloved pony Fairy. And her spirits could not help but be buoyed by the joy and reverence of the hundreds of Hawaiians — native and foreign-born alike — who came to call on her.

Still, seeing her people again brought her face to face with the misery and poverty that years of change and unrest had created. She wrote to her aunt,

> Last Sunday the Hawaiians came out to see me. There were several hundreds, and by six o'clock I didn't know what to do with myself, I was so tired. . . . It made me feel so sad to see so many of the Hawaiian people looking so poor. In the old days I am sure there were not so many people almost destitute.

Whether or not the monarchy was restored, there was so much for both Lili'uokalani and Ka'iulani to do to try to better the lives of all the Hawaiian people, to look out for those who were not the fortunate few in power.

Shortly after her return, Ka'iulani received a letter from Lili'uokalani, which her aunt had written almost immediately after their meeting. Eagerly, Ka'iulani sat down to read it — and once again, she was dismayed by her aunt's words. After a pleasant opening, Lili'uokalani said,

> I was glad to know that your heart and that of your father lay in

Kaʻiulani back home, comfortable again in a holokū

the right direction that is you are interested in the cause of your people.

Here is an opportunity for me to let you know something which I felt you ought to know — and I leave it for your own good judgement to guide you in your decision. It has been made known to me that it is the intention of the members of the Republican Government of Hawaiʻi to ask you to take the Throne of Hawaiʻi in the case they failed in their scheme of Annexation. That you should have nothing to say about the managing — that shall be theirs still, but you are to be a figurehead only. If you were to accept their proposition there would be no change whatever in the situation of the country for the good of the people or for all classes of men or for business advancements. You would only be in Mr. Dole's place, despised, and as he is now, in fear of his life.

You will have a few followers who will love you, but it will only be the 2,600 who now are supporting Dole's Government and still have over 80,000 opposing you. It is through their mismanagement that their government has not been a success. It is for this reason that knowing their instability they want to annex Hawaiʻi to America. Another reason why their Government has not been a success is that the people are not with them and they are fully aware of the fact. So as a last trial they wish you to take it. I have shown you in the above, the danger.

Liluʻuokalani went on to explain that if Kaʻiulani turned down the chance to be a "figurehead" queen under the control of the Republicans, it would only increase her popularity and weaken that of the Republic to the point of collapse. If at that juncture the people insisted on a popular election — open to all Hawaiians — and called for Kaʻiulani to be queen, Liliʻuokalani urged her to accept it as something "maintained by the love of the people." Liluʻuokalani continued,

I think Mr. T. H. Davies and George MacFarlane are knowing of this plan and I know approve of it. George said to me when I was in San Francisco that you and I ought to agree on this matter, that I ought to yield to you as the R. of Hawai'i, never to consent to have me reign again, that it were better if we agreed on you. I did not give him any answer because I had no right to. The people's wish is paramount with me, and what they say I abide by. Now my dear Child, for you are very dear to me, I hope you will act wisely for your own sake and be cautious in signing any documents they may present to you, reading over thoroughly and understanding it beforehand — for they are the greatest liars, and deceitful in all their undertakings and your young heart is too pure to see their wickedness. I mean the PGs. My Dear Niece, may the Almighty help you. Love to your father and I think it well you should show him this letter.

Although Lili'uokalani closed with "your affectionate aunt," Ka'iulani was distressed. Again she felt that her aunt suspected her of disloyalty. She had Theo Davies answer immediately:

I take the liberty of saying that neither Mr. Damon or Mr. MacFarlane or anyone else has ever conferred with me in regard to putting forward claims on behalf of Princess Ka'iulani to the Throne of Hawai'i. I am also certain that under no circumstances would the Princess Ka'iulani have accepted the Throne except with the approval of Your Majesty and at the joint request of Hawaiians and foreigners.

Yet it is interesting to note that Lili'uokalani did not ask Ka'iulani to decline the throne. Instead, she told Ka'iulani under what circumstances it would be politically wise for her to accept it.

For the first time, Liliʻuokalani had softened her stance, and stood willing to relinquish her claims in favor of her niece. And Theo Davies, in his reply, did not say that Kaʻiulani would never take the throne. He said she would take it only under the circumstances her aunt had described: in response to the will of the people, not in response to the connivings of the Republicans, who wanted her only as a figurehead.

Liliʻuokalani's assessment of the situation was accurate. The Republicans were vastly unpopular. Partly for this reason, they had to act with feigned cordiality toward the returned princess. They might imprison the stubborn queen, but they knew that if they touched the beloved princess, they risked the overwhelming wrath of the population.

Accordingly, Princess Kaʻiulani was invited everywhere by Royalists and Republicans alike — to the theater, to the galas, to sporting events. She attended, usually escorted by Prince Koa. Rumors about their supposed engagement were rampant.

The Republicans could outlaw Royalist meetings. But when the princess appeared at Cyclomere Park on the night of the bicycle-racing finals, the band spontaneously broke into "Hawaiʻi Ponoʻī," and the crowd leaped to their feet to pay her homage. How could the Republicans prohibit such unplanned tributes?

In fact, the only suspect public activity to which Kaʻiulani gave her support was a grand luʻau that raised considerable funds through those who attended. It was no coincidence that soon after this luʻau, a group of pro-royalty commissioners left for Washington to help battle the Annexation Treaty.

Their arrival helped fuel the resolve of the senators who were against annexation. The treaty languished in the Senate, clearly unable to get the two-thirds majority vote necessary to pass. In Hawaiʻi, almost everyone felt that the Republic, supported by so few

Feeding the peacocks at ʿĀinahau: Prince Koa, Eva Parker, Rose Cleghorn, and Princess Kaʿiulani (left to right)

and near economic collapse, could not sustain itself much longer without annexation. The tense waiting game continued.

*   *   *

WHILE KAʿIULANI HAD been away, her other aunt, Kalākaua's widow, the dowager queen Kapiʿolani, had suffered a series of strokes and was mostly confined to her Waikīkī home. Koa and Kūhiō — and Kūhiō's wife, Elizabeth — saw to her care. Now that Kaʿiulani was home, she visited as often as she could.

The young woman found that her two aunts, both former queens, had very different ideas and attitudes. Unlike Liliʿuokalani, who was certain the Hawaiian nation would be restored, Kapiʻolani felt sure it would not be. While Liliʻuokalani was angry and bitter, Kapiʻolani had made her peace with the future of her beloved islands. As she held the hand of her niece, she whispered, "For myself, I can only pray that God will bring Hawaiʻi a good future. I do not think I ought to tell Him how."

The former crown princess wished she could have either the peace and acceptance of the one queen or the fight and resolve of the other. As it was, her feelings rocked back and forth. Her hopes had been raised so often, only to be dashed. Even so, it was hard not to be hopeful when so many things seemed to point toward a possible restoration.

Kaʻiulani had thought it would be so much easier to be home, actively working to help her people. But she found their poverty overwhelming and other changes disconcerting. She admitted to Liliʻuokalani, "I should have written sooner, but writing is such a tax to my head here. I wonder why that is. I don't feel the least bit settled. I suppose it is because the old natives are all dead or married." She also added that she was suffering from the heat — in fact, she admitted that she now found the Hawaiian heat harder to bear than the English winters!

*   *   *

CHRISTMAS BROUGHT A series of festive balls, but Kaʻiulani had to summon her best acting abilities simply to appear cheerful.

Kaʻiulani *was* happy that she had re-established a warm relationship with Liliʻuokalani, and she felt relieved to have someone with whom she didn't have to pretend, with whom she could share her deepest feelings. In January she admitted, "The people of the Government are not particularly nice to me, excepting Mrs. Damon [wife of Samuel Damon, a member of the Republic's executive council] and Mrs. Dole. I think they are very sorry to see me here, especially as I give them no cause to complain. Thank God, Annexation is not a fact. The people here are not half so happy as when I first came back. I find everything so much changed."

On February 2, she gave a farewell lūʻau for Clive Davies, who was returning to England to be married. (The Davies had arrived for a visit several months earlier.) What fun it was to laugh at the former rumors and send dear Clive off in style! Not long after, Kaʻiulani bid farewell to Theo Davies and the rest of the family, who were also returning to Britain for the wedding.

On February 19, Kaʻiulani threw a huge lūʻau for Prince Koa's thirtieth birthday. Two hundred guests were invited for dinner. It was a grand occasion — the kind for which the new house had been built. The sit-down feast was sumptuous; the band played all evening. Partiers danced beneath colorful Chinese lanterns. After dinner, Koa rose and proposed a glowing toast to his hostess. In response, Archie rose and gave a warm toast to the prince. Many in attendance wondered if Archie was finally warming to the handsome Kawānanakoa, whose reputation with the ladies had bothered him in the past.

Ironically, while no one would have been surprised by the announcement of an engagement between the prince and the princess, after this party, Koa seldom escorted Kaʻiulani in public. Nevertheless, rumors continued to swirl about these two charismatic aliʻi, claiming one or the other had broken the other's heart. With their political enmity behind them, they seemed to settle into a comfortable friendship — or was there some truth to the rumors?

Years later, the princess's niece would claim that Kaʻiulani's relationship with Koa, while very close, was not romantic, but that of brother and sister. And yet Abigail Wahiikaahuula Campbell, who eventually became Koa's wife, candidly told a biographer that she could never have married Prince David had Kaʻiulani still been in the picture. The complicated truth could perhaps embrace both these observations.

Meanwhile, Kaʻiulani's name was linked with two worthy Englishmen, one a ship's captain, the other, Andrew Adams, a newspaper reporter and amateur actor who was considered quite a catch. Archie favored Andrew and did everything in his power to bolster the young man's suit. But Andrew and Kaʻiulani quarreled frequently, and the two finally parted company.

While the princess was undoubtedly the most eligible young woman in the Islands, and its citizens enjoyed speculation about her affections, she herself found it hard to concentrate on romance while her country — and her own role in its future — were as yet unsettled.

* * *

ON FEBRUARY 21, news arrived that the U.S. battleship *The Maine* had been sunk in the harbor of Havana, Cuba, reportedly on Spanish orders. No one could imagine how this faraway event would soon impact Hawaiʻi's future.

Hawaiians were more interested in the final defeat of the Annexation Treaty in the Senate. Annexationists scrambled to resubmit the treaty, this time to *both* Congress and the Senate, which would require only a simple majority to pass instead of the two-thirds majority it required when submitted to the Senate alone. They knew this was their last recourse, their very last chance. The native Hawaiians, meanwhile, were quietly exultant about the defeat. It seemed their long years of waiting would finally pay off.

* * *

"The Reluctant Bridegroom," a cartoon lampooning the "marriage"
of the United States and Hawaiʻi

LILIʻUOKALANI FINISHED WRITING her book in Washington,
and in March, copies of it arrived in the Islands. Her opinions in-
censed the Republicans, and even some Hawaiians. Representatives
of the Hui Aloha ʻĀina Society, who had visited her in Washington,
were quoted in the Honolulu papers as saying, "Queen Liliʻuokalani
only want money. She print a big book to sell for money for her-

self. . . . She did not help our delegation. We do not want her. We want our young Princess."

Although many readers scoffed that such educated men were quoted speaking "pidgin English," their sentiments seemed to have been truly relayed. The society did quickly mobilize its members to stand behind the princess.

Under the circumstances, Ka'iulani had probably quietly prepared to take the throne, in the event it was offered to her. In the privacy of her home, she had likely chosen her cabinet, testing the loyalty of old friends and the potential of the new. How could she have done otherwise?

In early April, Princess Ka'iulani attended a grand concert at the opera house in Honolulu to benefit the Kalihi and Moanalua churches. As had become customary, she and her party occupied the royal box on the right-hand side of the stage. President Dole and his party occupied the opposite box to the left of the stage.

As the lights dimmed, the featured singers of the evening, the Kawaihau Trio, bowed deeply to Ka'iulani and sang, in Hawaiian, a new song by Charles King. Its title was "Lei No Ka'iulani" — "A Wreath for Princess Ka'iulani." Members of the Republican government, most of whom had never taken the time to become fluent in Hawaiian, thought it was a sweet tribute in song.

Those who understood the lyrics, however, knew that in the most public of places, the singers were crowning their queen:

> Bring forth the wreath of lehua [the flower of the queen]
> The wreath for our beloved Princess.
> Loving hands with the maile didst weave
> A beautiful crown for Ka'iulani.
> And upon thy head we will place it,
> How lovely and charming to behold there.

Royal and queenly thou art,
Our loving Ka'iulani.
This token of love for thee we bring, oh receive it, Ka'iulani!
Wear your lei of yellow lehua
Entwined with the fragrant maile.

In other words, "Accept the crown! We offer it to you with love!"

At the end of the song, the audience rose to its feet as one, clapping and cheering.

At that moment, it seemed anything was possible.

* * *

A MONTH LATER, on May 1, U.S. admiral George Dewey sank the Spanish fleet in retaliation for the destruction of *The Maine*. The Spanish fleet had been stationed in Manila Bay in the Philippines.

Hawai'i, in the midst of the Pacific between the United States and the Philippines, suddenly became a strategic port for the American fleet.

The Republicans were thrilled to welcome the U.S. Navy, the "brave boys in blue," as they came to refuel to ready for war. Honolulu exploded in red, white, and blue bunting. The wives of the heads of government became the heads of the Red Cross (with Ka'iulani politely asked to be second vice-president). Hawai'i was suddenly swarming with U.S. sailors.

On May 25, Ka'iulani wrote to her Aunt Lili'uokalani, "I am sure you would be disgusted if you could see the way the town is decorated for the American troops. Honolulu is making a fool of itself and I only hope we won't all be ridiculed."

The island Americans burned with "war fever." Even Archie found it politic to open the grounds of 'Āinahau to the sailors. But on June 2, Kaʻiulani received news that distracted her. Theo Davies, the guardian who had become a second father to her, had died unexpectedly in England.

The princess was overwhelmed with sorrow. For days, Archie reported that she was "stunned and listless." It is not surprising that she reacted so strongly. She felt like she was losing everything and everyone that she loved. She remembered the words of her aunt at the death of her uncle: "If it is the father's will in Heaven, I must submit, for the Bible teaches us 'he doeth all things well.'"

But the Bible also taught that God "does not give us more than we can bear." How much more could she bear?

She was about to find out.

On July 13, the *S.S. Coptic* was sighted off Diamond Head. Using naval flags, the crew aboard flashed out the news they brought from the United States:

The Islands are annexed!

Hawaiʻi, U.S.A.!

Kaʻiulani — once "the little royal maid," now an ex-princess

TWELVE

Gone with the Tradewinds

The gentle voice roused her in the dead of night. "Ka'iulani Ali'i. Princess."

Ka'iulani pulled herself awake. "Yes?" she murmured.

"The call has come. She's almost here."

Ka'iulani sat up quickly, forcing herself to think. "Has the carriage been called for?"

"Yes, Your Highness."

Your Highness. A pretty title, and now, an empty one.

She chose a gown of black, and her maid quickly helped her dress.

Outside, large clouds veiled the night sky; moonlight filtered through only intermittently. The solemn ride down the Waikīkī road was dark; palm trees painted phantom figures in the light tradewinds.

As the carriage moved along, Ka'iulani could not help but remember her first midnight ride, when she had accompanied the body of her mother to the palace. This was again a funeral journey.

Lili'uokalani returned to Hawai'i and her people after the Annexationists were victorious.

It acknowledged the death of Hawai'i Nei ("Hawai'i, its own self").

The islanders now knew what had happened in Washington. The U.S. war in the Pacific had brought into sharp focus the military importance of the Hawaiian Islands. The Annexation Treaty, presumed dead, had been quickly revived and rushed through Congress. It had passed on the first vote.

Another carriage came into sight ahead of Ka'iulani's, and soon another and another. As they traveled, silent figures on foot joined the flow in clusters.

By the time they reached the dock, hundreds of ghostlike mourners were already there. In the torchlight, Ka'iulani saw Koa near the front of the throng.

The ship *Gaelic* sliced through the waves like a tall black shadow. After it had docked and let down its gangplank, Koa boarded with a few others and disappeared into a shelter that had been raised on board. Within a few moments, he appeared again.

On his arm was ex-queen Liliʻuokalani. In silence she walked regally across the deck. No band played; no cheers or applause greeted her. Instead, she stood tall at the top of the gangplank and spoke one word:

"Aloha!"

As one, the throng returned her greeting: *A-lo-ha!*

And then she was among them, and the tears flowed. It seemed as though everyone wept. The older Hawaiians began the death wail. It rose and fell with the tide.

Kaʻiulani shivered. It was her worst nightmare, replaying itself. Only this time she was awake.

The crowd parted before Liliʻuokalani as she walked with her entourage to the royal carriage. Kaʻiulani descended to meet her aunt, and the two women embraced. Then Koa helped them back up into the carriage and climbed aboard himself.

The next day, Kaʻiulani found that the haole papers reported simply that "Mrs. Dominis returned home."

The Hawaiian version was far more memorable.

When the royal carriage had arrived at Washington Place, the queen's home, Kaʻiulani and Koa had excused themselves and gone to the morning room while Liliʻuokalani changed and ate dinner.

The prince and princess, who had gone through so much together, found little to say to each other as they waited.

When Liliʻuokalani was ready, the doors to her home were opened. The Hawaiians entered, one at a time, crawling across the floor on their knees, to kiss the hand of their queen. The reverence and love evident in that simple gesture conveyed the entire story of a country lost.

No matter what some faraway Congress said, Liliʻuokalani was still their queen.

It was, as one writer said, as if they'd come to weep at the bier of Hawaiʻi. And, Kaʻiulani thought, as if her aunt was the widow, and she and Koa the next of kin.

She did not return to ʻĀinahau until dawn.

* * *

KAʻIULANI HATED PLAYING the invalid, but she had not felt strong for quite a while. She had planned to get away to the Parker Ranch for some respite from the cauldron of high emotions in Honolulu, but had remained at home to greet her aunt. For the next two weeks, she stayed at ʻĀinahau as much as possible, choosing to keep her grief private.

Annexation Day was set for August 12. On the day itself, she dressed in a beautiful black gown with a fitted bodice and intricate needlework. Her long hair was captured in combs at the back of her head; she wore a tufted lei of oʻo feathers, the symbol of highest Hawaiian aliʻi.

At the appointed hour, she rode down Waikīkī Road into Honolulu. Again, many people were heading for the palace. But unlike the day of King Kalākaua's coronation, the skies were hung with gray clouds. And among those heading for the palace, there were no Hawaiians.

Kaʻiulani was not going to the palace, either. Instead, her carriage followed back streets to Washington Place. There, with Liliʻuokalani, Koa, and their inner circle, they laid to rest the sovereign nation that had been Hawaiʻi.

Only two blocks away at the government building (ʻIolani Palace), President Dole was handing over control of the Republic of Hawaiʻi to U.S. minister Harold M. Sewall.

As one witness reported, "'Hawai'i Pono'ī' was being played as the Hawaiian flag was lowered for the last time. Before it ended, the native musicians threw down their instruments and ran away, around the corner of the Palace . . . to weep in private."

By all accounts, the ceremony was subdued. It seemed even the men who had worked so hard for this day knew that for many others it was a time of great sorrow. Something had been gained, yes, but something had also been lost for good.

*   *   *

ONCE ANNEXATION WAS a fact, Ka'iulani and Lili'uokalani had little time to grieve. The battlefield might have changed, but the fight for control of the country was not over.

The members of the former Republican government (most of whom retained their positions and continued running the new territory of Hawai'i until Congress enacted a permanent form of government) wanted to keep the same voting restrictions. The Hawaiians wanted universal (male) suffrage.

Both Lili'uokalani and Ka'iulani were quick to see that at least some good might come of the Americanization. If they won voting rights for all, native Hawaiians would be given back their voice.

On the heels of annexation, the United States sent two senators — Shelby Collum of Iowa and John Morgan of Alabama — and a congressman — Robert Hitt — as commissioners to Hawai'i. Their job was to assess the new territory and make recommendations for its governance, with the help of acting president Sanford Dole and Hawaiian Supreme Court justice Walter Frear.

Every special-interest group in the Islands clamored to have their say. The Republicans were again claiming that the natives were uneducated savages, unworthy of the vote.

Annexation Day: the lowering of the Hawaiian flag (above) and the raising of the American flag in front of ʻIolani Palace (below)

During the annexation ceremonies at the palace (above), mourners gathered at Washington Place (below): Liliʻuokalani is seated; Koa and Kaʻiulani stand on her right

It was up to the former queen and crown princess to prove them wrong.

* * *

LILIʻUOKALANI'S PLAN WAS simple yet effective. When the American commissioners announced plans to visit the outer islands, she announced a similar trip.

Wherever the commissioners went, they received a polite greeting. But shortly thereafter, Liliʻuokalani would arrive, and the Hawaiians would drop everything to pay her homage.

The message was clear.

At one point the commissioners and their party arrived at the Volcano House on the mountain of Moana Kea to find that all the accommodations had been assigned to the former queen. They accepted the situation with good grace, and even spent a cordial evening socializing with Liliʻuokalani. They found her to be a warm and cultured woman, not simply the political enemy the Republicans had painted her to be.

* * *

THE FORMER REPUBLICANS did everything in their power to keep the commissioners from attending "native" functions.

However, when the invitation came for a grand dinner to be given by Princess Kaʻiulani at her Waikīkī estate on September 7, no one could find an objection. The commissioners happily accepted.

Kaʻiulani felt that this was the answer to her prayers for wisdom about how she could help her people. She also knew that this was the "state dinner" for which she had been trained, and for which the new house had been built.

This was her best chance to prove that Hawaiians had their own culture and traditions, yes — but that didn't make them savages! Ka'iulani rallied every ounce of her strength and ingenuity to do her people proud.

The evening was carefully planned. Congressman Hitt, along with senators Morgan and Collum and their wives and friends, arrived to find a splendid fairyland. Colored lanterns dotted the estate, and a military band was jauntily playing popular songs of the day.

The princess, their hostess, wore a beautifully brocaded, yellow satin holokū, with a royal leī of o'o feathers around her neck. The other guests, many native Hawaiians, wore the finest clothes and greeted the commissioners cordially. It was an American's dream of paradise: cultured but exotic.

Ka'iulani had planned meticulously so that the spell would deepen as the evening continued. When dinner was announced, the guests moved in a double line, as they'd been partnered, to three tables, each set with forty places. Ka'iulani, on Senator Collum's arm, led the way.

The guests' first surprise was a happy one: leī of carnations or maile (fragrant green leaves) at each place. Their next discoveries were more alarming to some of them.

According to the seating arrangements, the Americans sat side by side with native Hawaiians. And the food set before them was traditional Hawaiian fare — right down to the calabashes of poi! They took this in, then looked up to find kāhili bearers stationed behind the chairs of each of the royals — Ka'iulani, Lili'uokalani, and Kawānanakoa (one at each table) — waving the tall, feathered sticks above their ali'i.

After the blessing, the princess with the soft English accent smiled at Mrs. Collum, then daintily dipped her fingers into the poi bowl at her table.

The lavish "state dinner" hosted by Kaʻiulani at ʻĀinahau. Kaʻiulani is seated near the end of the main table, flanked by kāhili bearers.

Mrs. Collum was aghast. This wasn't a formal dinner party at all. It was a native lūʻau! Heaven only knew *what* they'd be eating!

But Mrs. Hitt was smitten with the whole effect. Following Kaʻiulani's lead, she too dipped her fingers into the poi and ate happily without a spoon.

With the tension broken, the feasting began in earnest. Senator Collum was among the first to fill a heaping plate.

Hearty conversation and laughter soon filled the night as the commissioners found the Hawaiians to be educated, interesting dinner companions.

After the feast, the tables were cleared from the lānai so the band could again take its place. Then the dancing began — a senator partnered with the queen, a congressman with the princess, and their wives taking turns with the dashing Hawaiian prince. At the end of the party, the Americans had to admit that, although they'd experienced Hawaiian culture — and waltzed with native Hawaiians — they certainly had seen no barbaric practices! These people were certainly as capable of casting a fair vote as the former Republicans!

The evening was a huge success. Ka'iulani could rightly feel that when her people had needed her, she had risen to the challenge.

*　*　*

FOR A MONTH, from mid-September to October 12, Ka'iulani allowed herself a short getaway. She went to stay with her half-sister Helen and her family up in the Manoa Valley. After all the summer's events, it was a much-needed rest.

She returned to 'Āinahau and the social season in time for her twenty-third birthday on October 16.

Two days later, Ka'iulani and her father hosted a reception for two hundred people, and the following week, 'Āinahau was the scene of a gala dancing party. The social season finally wound down, and Ka'iulani gave a sigh of relief as she hosted her last "at home."

*　*　*

ONCE THE COMMISSIONERS left, Lili'uokalani made plans to return to Washington as well. She planned to continue to fight for native Hawaiian rights and for compensation for all the Crown lands (property that belonged personally to the monarch) that had been taken from her.

A great crowd of people again gathered to wish the queen farewell. Her longtime advisor, Colonel MacFarlane (who had advised Lili'uokalani to give up the throne in favor of Ka'iulani), was there. He wrote about the occasion in detail:

The boat was delayed, and although the hour was late and

Kaʻiulani delicate she refused to leave, and stayed on board some five hours to see the last of her aunt. Any heart must have been touched at the sight of those two royal women clinging together in their fallen dignity. I was trying to console Kaʻiulani with some cheerful prospects.

"All has not been taken from you," I said. "The American Government respects your position and will help you to keep it up. . . . You will still be able to live as an ex-Princess; your birth and your antecedents will never be forgotten, and you will remain a leader of society here, the first lady in the land."

"Yes," she answered me with a tired smile, "but I shan't be much of a real Princess, shall I? They haven't left me much to live for. . . . I try not to grieve my father, who watches over me so devotedly and seeks to make up to me for all I have lost. For his sake, I try not to mind, to appear bright and happy. But I think my heart is broken."

Before the end of the the month, Kaʻiulani wrote a frank and poignant letter to her aunt:

Daily we as a great race are being subjected to a great deal of misery and the more I see of American soldiers about town, the more I am unable to tolerate them, what they stand for and the way we are belittled it is enough to ruin one's faith in God.

Last week some Americans came to the house and knocked rather violently at the door, and when they had stated their cause, they wished to know if it would be permissible for the EX-princess to have her picture taken with them. Oh, will they never leave us alone? They have now taken away everything from us and it seems there is left but little, and that little our very life itself. . . .

The main entrance to ʻĀinahau, no longer the home it had once been for Kaʻiulani

We live in such a semi-retired way . . . that people wonder if
we even exist any more. I wonder, too, and to what purpose?

Kaʻiulani needed a happy distraction. She knew her father
hoped that Andrew Adams, her former beau, would provide exactly
that when he returned to ʻĀinahau on holiday. But she was in no
mood for romance.

Instead, she had her sights set on a wonderful occasion that would
allow her to get away. Her old friend Eva Parker was getting married at
her family's ranch on the Big Island. Kaʻiulani remembered what happy
times she and her mother had had on their "escapes" to the island of
Hawaiʻi. With the closest thing to joy she'd felt in a long while, she began to pack.

A still-regal Ka'iulani poses for the camera

THIRTEEN

A Final Purpose

For Kaʻiulani, it was a great relief to leave Oʻahu for the Big Island. Here, no churches were used as spy towers (as Central Union Church had been during the overthrow); the towns were not swarming with brash young American soldiers; sons of missionaries did not insult her people by calling them savages.

Here, instead, were the wide-open acres of the Parker Ranch, a close group of friends, and an island full of Hawaiians who adored their aliʻi.

Kaʻiulani had known the Parker girls since childhood. Not only had she spent time at their ranch when she was a little girl, but she had enjoyed outings with Helen and Eva in London. They shared an understanding of different worlds. Once Kaʻiulani had felt inferior to the older, more cultured Parker girls, but time and experience had made her feel like one of their peers.

The ranch itself covered thousands of acres of the Big Island, encompassing craggy mountains, rolling pasturelands, and beaches.

A view of the Parker Ranch on the Big Island

The most famous *paniolo* (cowboys) in Hawai'i worked for Sam Parker.

Sam Parker was a generous host, and he stinted on nothing for his daughter Eva's wedding. The gathered guests were treated to parties, dances, picnics, and many other entertainments. Other prominent Big Island families also hosted grand dinners in honor of Eva and her fiancé.

Ka'iulani was happier than she had been for a long time. She very much enjoyed the assembled group, including Sam Woods, a cousin of the Parkers. He usually was her escort, even though Prince Koa was also one of the guests.

The wedding was celebrated in mid-December; the guests were welcome to stay on through Christmas, and many did — including Ka'iulani.

In early January, Ka'iulani decided to extend her visit, as she had so delighted in doing as a child. She wrote to Archie on January 6:

Dearest Pa,

Many thanks for your letter. I am glad to know you have been enjoying yourself. You seem quite gay with your reception for the officers. . . .

Of course I don't mind lending 'Āinahau to any of our own friends. I only regret I won't be there to attend the reception. We are all well and it goes without saying we are enjoying ourselves immensely —

We had more than enough fun at the Ball in Waimea. All the people were in their best clothes, and had on their best manners. The Jarretts asked us to it, and they provided supper for our party, and very good it was too. I did not dance very much as I was too amused watching the Country Bumpkins. . . .

It had been raining all that day (Friday) and Saturday we could not see twenty yards away — the fog was so thick. We left that evening for Mana [the ranch] in spite of the weather. My goodness the rain cut one's face . . . and it was blowing like cats and dogs. We got home at 7:30, wet to the skin, but thanks to a warm bath and warm drink and dinner, we were none the worse for it. . . .

Tuesday we rode over to Waipio, got there about 3:30 p.m. There were quite a number of natives called and during the evening the natives came and serenaded us. . . . The next morning we took a ride around the valley, unfortunately it began to rain so I had no time to see my land or rather our land. I am sorry as I would have liked to have seen it.

We had to hurry as Lumaheihei was afraid of the Pali being too slippery. I never rode up such a place in all my life. I was simply hanging on by my teeth. We had a splendid ride home, jumping logs and pig holes. . . .

David goes down on the Kinau today to bring up the Dowager. . . .

I want you to send me my money for the month, what is left and also the $40 for January — I may not need it, but I want to have it any way. Please don't forget.

Merry Christmas to you all. My Love to the family. I am so very sorry Helen has been so seedy. What was the matter with her? Tell Elsie to send up my holokus without fail. I want them badly. Send me up some Bromo Quinine pills, also get me headache powders No. 75618 from Hollister —

Our love to you all, and with much for yourself from,

Your loving,

VIKE

P.S. Koa will tell you all news.

As this letter shows, Kaʻiulani continued to put on a happy face for her father; the added request to send pills and headache powders was the only hint that she still wasn't feeling strong.

*   *   *

IN MID-JANUARY, SOME of the friends who had stayed on at the ranch decided to go horseback riding up into the mountains; the princess was one of them. They were well along the trail when the sun disappeared behind gray clouds. Quickly thereafter, a cold, driving rain began relentlessly pelting the riders.

With excited shouts, the riders pulled rain slickers from their saddle rolls and stopped their horses, planning to turn back.

All except Kaʻiulani.

The last photograph ever taken of Kaʻiulani (left),
on the steps of the Parker home

The others called to the princess to put on her coat. Some sources say that, even as Kaʻiulani refused her raingear, she saw an old kahuna on the path before her. Not wanting to meet him, she urged her mount to a gallop and rode up into the storm. Others say it was simply a move reminiscent of her spirited rebellion years ago, when she ran from Miss Gardinier back into the ocean, that caused her to recklessly head up into the mountains.

The others felt they had no choice but to follow.

By the time they returned to Mana, Kaʻiulani was thoroughly soaked.

No one thought much of the adventure (they had, after all, recently been soaked to the skin several times, and been none the worse for it) until the princess awoke the next day feeling "seedy." By January 24, her illness was reported in the Honolulu papers.

Archie sailed for Mana and brought the family physician, Dr. Walters, who diagnosed Kaʻiulani as suffering from inflammatory rheumatism. However, within a couple of weeks she was well enough to be carried down to the steamer to return home. By then, the pain lingered only in the left side of her head and in her left forearm.

Kaʻiulani was sorry to leave the Big Island. She'd felt happy there, and free to be herself. On the other hand, it was a relief to be back at ʻĀinahau, in her own room. Dr. Walters predicted she would be up and around in a matter of days. Papa hovered, and her half-sister Helen (herself recovered) came to help run the household. Kaʻiulani was well enough to sit up in bed and chat with close friends about news from town.

"Look at this!" Papa said one day, huffing at the newspapers as usual. *The Advertiser* had run a long article about the new petition being sent to Washington, requesting that the new government continue to give a yearly stipend to the dethroned princess. What indicated that virtually everyone was in favor of granting this petition was the fact that it was signed solely by the only individuals who might have voiced an objection — the members of the original P.G.s.

Archie went on to read, "The quiet efforts of Princess Kaʻiulani to obliterate the harsh feelings growing out of the change of government in Hawaiʻi, and her acceptance of the new order of things, is appreciated by this community. And by none more so than those who were directly instrumental in bringing that change about. . . . Whether the object of the petition is successful or not, it is a strong tribute by active political opponents to the character and worth of Kaʻiulani."

"Well!" said Archie, his voice showing more emotion than he expressed in words. "It's about time!"

Ka'iulani lay back on her pillows. So even the political enemies who had once feared her now paid tribute to her strength of character. It somehow felt like a mixed blessing to be the personification of the meeting point of two factions, Hawaiian and Western. Yet, she herself was just that.

*   *   *

DR. WALTERS DIDN'T understand why Ka'iulani wasn't improving; in fact, she appeared to be getting worse. He called in a colleague, and although they added the diagnosis of an exophthalmic goiter (an eye problem) to the original diagnosis, they were more concerned about the rheumatism, which seemed to be attacking Ka'iulani's already weakened heart. She tried to remain cheerful in her talks with her friends Kate and Helen and her family, but she was so tired . . . so very tired.

By the end of February, the doctors were increasingly worried about her condition. Still, they felt she had a fair chance of recovery — she was, after all, only twenty-three years old.

On Sunday, March 5, the doctors told the press, "The Princess rested better on Saturday night. She was able to get a little sleep. She had a bad turn Sunday morning, but as the day progressed there was an improvement. . . . Altogether it can be said the young lady is slightly better, but not yet entirely out of danger."

Indeed she was not.

Just after midnight, as Sunday crept into Monday, the princess took a turn for the worse. She fought for breath, and her fragile heart drummed, trying to pump needed oxygen into the blood. Her alarmed physicians called the retainers and had the family members roused from their beds. Archie and his daughters Helen and Rosie rushed to Ka'iulani's bedside immediately; within the hour they were joined by Kaʻiulani's closest friends — Kate Vida, Helen Parker, and Prince Koa.

Each person in the room was stunned by the thought of losing her, but it was perhaps hardest for "papa." Archie would give anything to make her stay. But he knew her losses had been so many and so great: her mother, her sister, her adopted father, her country. She had felt the death of Theo Davies so keenly that Archie knew his death had symbolized all that was truly gone for her, all that would never be. A century was passing, a country was gone. Perhaps God had made her for this country and this time. Perhaps it was fitting she should go as well. Archie touched her dear face and brushed her coal-black hair. He had welcomed her into this world. Now he must let her go.

Kaʻiulani's breathing became more labored, but she struggled to continue. She knew that those in the room were terrified at the prospect of losing her, but she herself was calm about her approaching death. She felt she had done all she could; she had given her heart to her people and her energy to their cause. She simply had nothing left to give. She was ready to lay down the only crown she still had at the foot of the King of Kings.

At precisely two A.M., she stirred, and through a parched throat called out a single word. It was so garbled that even those around her bed could not agree on what it was. Did she call out for her mother? her father? Koa?

Then Kaʻiulani sank back onto the pillows. She was gone.

At the moment of her death, Kaʻiulani's peacocks began an unearthly screeching that woke people for miles around. Said one friend, "We heard them miles away, and we knew the Princess had died."

Added *The Advertiser:* "And there passed away she who was the most beloved of the Hawaiian race."

"The Last Respects Paid to a Gentle Aliʻi": *The Advertiser* announces Kaʻiulani's death

*   *   *

ALL AROUND THE Islands, news of Kaʻiulani's death fell like a physical blow as stunning as that of the overthrow. The collective grief was so great and so deeply felt that it was said that everyone felt as if they'd lost a close member of their own family.

Overnight the morticians came, bringing a white coffin. The young princess was beautifully dressed in a robe of white and laid to rest on a bier in the grand parlor of her new house, facing the sea.

215

Despite all that the P.G.s had taken from her, they had at least been able to make a small overture of reconciliation before she died. The rest of the Westerners — and even more, of course, the native Hawaiians — were openly grieving.

When the doors of the house were opened the next day, the lines of mourners filed in, visibly stricken. This last visit to Kaʻiulani at her beloved ʻĀinahau was the first occasion on which everyone — from members of the former Republican government to native Hawaiian activists — came together for one purpose. There were no recriminations, no accusations. Only a shared sorrow. Outside, the band played dirges, native Hawaiians sang their meles of tribute or wailed the death chant, and groups of mourners clustered together, sobbing.

After the public viewing, the Cleghorn retainers, many of whom had served the princess from the time she was a baby, were allowed to pay their last respects.

Finally, Archie went into the room alone. Even the kāhili bearers were sent out. Before the white coffin adorned with white orchids and pure white orange blossoms, he said his final, private good-bye to his beloved daughter. After fifteen minutes, he emerged, clearly grief-stricken. Kaʻiulani's casket was then carried outside for the midnight ride to Kawaihahaʻo Church.

There, with Kaʻiulani lying in state, thousands of others said their final farewell.

Said the Western press: "Everyone admired her attitude. They could not do otherwise. Her dignity, her pathetic resignation, her silent sorrow appealed to all. The natives loved her for her quiet, steadfast sympathy with their woe, her uncomplaining endurance of her own; the whites admired her for her stately reserve, her queenly display of all necessary courtesy while holding herself aloof from undue intimacy. It was impossible not to love her."

And at the funeral, Pastor H. H. Parker added in his native lan-

The interior of Kawaihaha'o Church, decorated for Ka'iulani's funeral

Kaʻiulani's funeral procession. Throngs of mourners lined the streets.

guage, Hawaiian: "I want to add my flower to her wreath, the same as I am sure does every parent and every child in Hawaiʻi Neʻi. Love is a flower transplanted from Heaven, and all who knew Kaʻiulani loved her. . . . In your lives, follow her example."

The funeral and the funeral procession were an as yet unheard-of mixture of the mourning of all races. At the service, Sanford Dole and his cabinet members sat across from Hawaiian aliʻi. Immigrants from Japan and Portugal, China and the Philippines wept openly along the processional route. Once rivals, Prince Koa and Andrew Adams joined together as pall bearers. They were two of the 230 men who pulled Kaʻiulani's coffin on its catafalque during the two-hour journey from the church to the royal tomb at Nuʻuanu. All the while, guns boomed and bells tolled, as they had when the frightened young princess had accompanied her uncle the King during Queen Emma's funeral, as they had when the heart broken young woman had followed the casket of her mother. This time the funeral was hers, and the grief was left to others.

Because Kaʻiulani was half-Western and half-Hawaiian, it was

218

Ka'iulani's final resting place: the royal crypt at Nu'uanu

these two groups that were most deeply stricken. The Hawaiians' heartrending, chanted grief gave voice to everyone's great loss.

Up at Nu'uanu, beyond the iron gates where only a few were allowed to follow, the Episcopal bishop Willis read the Order for the Burial of the Dead.

And so Ka'iulani was laid to rest. She had indeed fought the good fight, having steadfastly refused to lead her people in the ways of hatred and violence. She had deplored injustice and had fought against it by trying to lead all peoples forward in love.

The next year would bring the turning of a new century. It would bring the Organic Act, which gave back to native Hawaiians the full rights of citizenship. It would bring the beginning of a new world. The old was gone. The new was come. Only the bridge between the two had been sacrificed.

*   *   *

KAʻIULANI'S SUITOR ANDREW Adams never got over his love for the princess. For many decades, a solitary figure brought flowers to the tomb at Nuʻuanu.

Yet he was far from the only loyal subject whose love for Kaʻiulani and respect for her beloved Hawaiʻi lived on.

Despite Kaʻiulani's death, her legacy of the spirit of aloha is very much alive. To this day there is a tangible, unique feeling of love and acceptance that thrives in the Islands.

My Sources for This Book

Any biographer is blessed when her subject lived in a time when people wrote letters and kept journals. She is twice blessed when that subject was deemed important enough that her letters and journals were kept. Archie Cleghorn kept every letter from his wife and daughter — even angry letters in which his wife threatened to leave him! Many of these are part of the Cleghorn Collection at the Hawaiian State Archives.

I owe a great *mahalo* to the help and aloha spirit of the librarians at the State Archives, where many personal records are kept; and the Bishop Museum, which houses priceless materials from the time period I researched, including the P.G.s' tracts and anti-royalty literature, as well as the handwritten *Kilo Kilo* books of the last monarchs. Great belated thanks also to David Kittelson at the University of Hawai'i for ferreting out rare books, magazines, and actual newspapers of the day. Holding a newspaper in your hands is somehow very different from reading it on microfilm. That said, the microfilm collection at the State Library was also immensely helpful.

Thanks also to the Friends of ʻIolani Palace, whose tireless efforts at restoration have preserved the feeling of the Kalākaua dynasty for generations to come.

No thanks would be complete without the acknowledgment of those who have gone before me. I owe a debt of gratitude to Kristin Zambucka, whose love of the Hawaiian culture shines through all of her photo biographies, including the one of Princess Kaʻiulani; she also did readers a great service by finding and passing along the letters Kaʻiulani wrote to Toby de Courcy, which reveal the princess's strong, distinctive voice.

We are all perhaps in greatest debt to Nancy and Jean Webb, who first pulled together all the disparate pieces of information on the princess for their (sadly, out of print) biography, *Kaiulani: Crown Princess of Hawaii*. They worked at a time when many of those who had known the princess were still alive; they felt most blessed to have been loaned the journals of Gertrude Gardinier.

I personally am indebted to this one-of-a-kind couple — not only for their incredible library of Hawaiian books and the happy hours we spent discussing "our princess," but for the friendship they offered to my husband and me, their tales of the "writing life" in the old days, their deeply ingrained love of the Hawaiian Islands, and the example they set by their obvious appreciation of and devotion to each other, even as Nancy's health failed. Neither will be forgotten.

Suggestions for Further Reading

Many wonderful books on Hawai'i are being published all the time. I'm sorry to have room to list only a few. Although some of these books are out of print, many of them are still in library circulation.

Bailey, Paul Dayton. *Those Kings and Queens of Old Hawaii*. Los Angeles: Westernlore Books, 1975.

A history of Hawai'i leading up to Ka'iulani's time that provides fascinating, in-depth stories of its colorful monarchs.

Daws, Gavan. *The Shoals of Time*. New York: Macmillan, 1968.

A comprehensive look at Hawai'i's history.

Field, Isobel. *This Life I've Loved.* New York: Longmans, 1940.

Robert Louis Stevenson's daughter shares memories of the time her family spent in Hawaiʻi in the 1880s.

Joesting, Edward. *Hawaii: An Uncommon History.* New York: W. W. Norton, 1972.

A well-documented history of the Islands.

Kuykundall, Ralph Simpson. *Hawaii: A History, from Polynesian Kingdom to American State.* Englewood Cliffs, N.J.: Prentice-Hall, 1961.

A well-respected, in-depth history of Hawaiʻi.

Liliʻuokalani. *Hawaiʻi's Story by Hawaiʻi's Queen.* Rutland, Vermont: Charles E. Tuttle Co., 1985.

A reprinting of the book first published by Liliʻuokalani in 1898. An interesting view of her side of the story.

Loomis, Albertine. *For Whom Are the Stars?* Honolulu: University of Hawaiʻi Press, 1976.

The story of the overthrow of Queen Liliʻuokalani, an intriguing pulling-together of many strands of the story.

Webb, Nancy, and Jean Francis Webb. *The Hawaiian Islands: From Monarchy to Democracy.* New York: Viking Press, 1956.

An engrossing history of Hawaiʻi — if you can find it!

————. *Kaiulani: Crown Princess of Hawaii.* New York: Viking Press, 1962.

A biography written before several key documents were available, but full of wonderful, vivid detail.

Zambucka, Kristin. *Princess Kaiulani: The Last Hope of Hawaii's Monarchy.* Honolulu: Mana Publishing Company, 1982.

A lovely book of photographs, complete with texts of letters and newspaper articles.

Photo Credits

The image on p. 2 is by Paul Emmert, courtesy of the Hawaii State Archives.

The photographs on pp. 4, 7, 8, 13, 16, 22, 24, 27, 33, 36, 42, 48, 50, 53, 55, 57, 58, 61, 66, 68, 69, 71, 74, 76, 81, 84, 86, 88, 92, 93, 96, 103, 106, 109, 111, 113, 116, 119, 124, 128, 136, 141, 143 (above), 145, 148, 152, 156, 159 (both photos), 172, 174, 180, 184, 192, 194, 198 (both photos), 199 (above), 202, 205, 215, 217, 218, 219 are supplied courtesy of the Hawaii State Archives.

The photographs on the cover, the frontispiece, pp. 18, 28, 30, 32, 38, 39, 85, 95, 154, 178, 199 (below), 206 are reproduced with permission from the Bernice P. Bishop Museum.

The images on pp. 6 and 45 are reproduced with permission from North Wind Picture Archive.

The photographs on pp. 100 (1995/631) and 101 (1994/284/29) are reproduced with permission from the Société Jersiaise Photographic Archive, Jersey, Channel Islands, UK.

Index

description of, 31; political in-
volvement of, 43-44, 62, 63, 97-98,
99; Republicans and, 157-58
Cleghorn, Helen, 24, 71
Cleghorn, Rose, 24, 71
Cleghorn, Thomas, 23
Cleghorn, Victoria Kawēkiu Lunalilo
Kalaninuiahilapalapa Kaʻiulani. *See*
Kaʻiulani, Princess
Cleveland, Frances Folsom, 129, 133
Cleveland, Grover, 118-19, 125, 130,
131-33, 144, 145, 146, 153
Colburn, John, 108
Collum, Shelby, 197, 201, 202
Committee of Safety, 108, 110
Cook, James, 11
Cosalo y Cisneros, Evangelina, 173
Crystal Palace, 78
Cummins, "Uncle John," 20

Damien, Father, 70-71
Damon, Mrs., 185-86
Damon, Samuel, 186
Davies, Alice, 95, 99, 103, 117
Davies, Clive, 95, 125, 127, 139, 142,
186
Davies, Mrs., 117
Davies, Theo: arrival in New York,
117-18; background of, 83; death
of, 191, 214; John Stevens and,
101; Kaʻiulani's education and, 99;
Koa and, 120-21; Liliʻuokalani
and, 182-83; relationship with
Kaʻiulani, 94-95; response to coup,
114-15; Washington interviews of,
129

de Courcy, Nevinson, 160, 162,
168
Dewey, George, 190
Diamond Head Charlie, 20, 32, 36
Diana, Princess, 127
Dole, George, 113
Dole, Mrs., 186
Dole, Sanford, 111, 113-14, 146,
196, 197, 218
Dominis, John Owen, 17, 25, 59,
89, 96-97
Dreghorn Castle, 94

Emma, Queen, 14, 33-34
Examiner, The, 176

Fairy, 20
Four Sacred Ones of Hawaiʻi, The,
16, 17, 64
Frear, Walter, 197
French Riviera, 158

Gardinier, Gertrude: engagement
of, 48-49; relationship with
Kaʻiulani, 35-36, 41, 45-46, 54,
56, 60, 72; trial period of, 30-32
Gibson, Walter Murray, 44, 49, 51,
62
Grand Bazaar, 165-67
Great Harrowden Hall, 79, 92, 99

Harrison, Benjamin, 118
Havana, 187
Hawaiʻi: annexation of, 168, 169,
191; class lines in, 10; counter-
revolution in, 155-56; death rate